Where Are The Sons In The House?

Dedicated to my spiritual father
Pastor Jimmy Crompton

Where Are The Sons In The House?

**Dedicated to my spiritual father
Pastor Jimmy Crompton**

By Jerome Nel

DESTINY IMAGE EUROPE
Via Maiella, 1
66020 San Giovanni Teatino (Ch) - Italy

ISBN:88-89127-01-5

First printing: 2004

This book and all other Destiny Image Europe books are available at Christian bookstores and distributors worldwide.

To order products, or for any other correspondence:

Tel. +39 085 4716623 - Fax: +39 085 4710868
E-mail: info@eurodestinyimage.com

Or reach us on the Internet:
www.eurodestinyimage.com

Acknowledgements

Thank you to the following wonderful people in my life. You have been vitally instrumental in the success of this book. However, even the most eloquent words or passionate declarations of my gratitude will never adequately express my deep sense of appreciation.

To my incredible wife, Lynne—Darling, without you by my side, I would be nothing. Thank you for encouraging me, coaxing me, and loving me no matter what. You've always been there like a pillar of strength in my life. You're the greatest gift that Jesus ever gave me.

To Rob and Felicity Wilson—Thank you for your untiring dedication to seeing this project through. You have sacrificed and labored unselfishly with me, sometimes through the night. You have served to the limit and never once complained. I love you for this.

To Pastor Tristan Deutschmann, a son in my house—Your dependability is unsurpassed. How humble, honest, and committed you are.

To the congregation of Garden Route Christian Centre—It is my privilege to be your Pastor. My world is richer and I walk taller for knowing you.

To Andre van der Merwe and Marni Albon, who are responsible for the great work on the cover. Thank you.

To Isaiah Laubscher, ace model on the cover.

Foreword

The church in the Old Testament was birthed as a family. Abraham, the father of all who believe, was called to start a holy nation. We are his spiritual sons. The Old Testament church, which is a shadow of the new, was the family nation of Israel. The shadow is a carbon copy of the real substance. Therefore, every believer becomes a member of the family of God.

This concept is practically never taught today. The New Testament speaks of the church as a holy (family) nation. But it also calls us the body of Christ, the temple (house of deity) of the Holy Spirit and the bride of Christ. But in the Old Testament all we see is a family nation (church). Just as praise and worship is thoroughly explained in the Old Testament and not given much emphasis in the New Testament, so the church as the family of God is very thoroughly dealt with and reproduced in the Old Testament, but not emphasized in the New Testament. Both the family nation and praise and worship are nevertheless just as important in the New Testament.

The tragedy is that the concept of the church as a family, with its inherent structure, commitment, and discipline, is unknown to most Christians. The concept of having a spiritual father has only recently come to the surface. The Bible repeatedly says that Abraham is our father. Only God can create the seed that carries His life, but He fathers us through other people.

I believe that the church, as a family, is the heart of New Testament discipleship. Jesus said, "Go and make disciples." I believe Jesus to be saying, "Go and build spiritual families" because that is what discipleship is all about.

I pray that the teaching in this book will change your life and that of your congregation so that Jesus Christ can truly be Lord, and that, as a result, we can enjoy the favor of the Father—the favor that flows from the Father to the children when we follow Him, trust Him, love Him, and live in unity within His house.

Why is it still unacceptable to some that the "father-heart of God" should be revealed through fathers?

This book will challenge the very roots of this problem. I pray that you will allow the Spirit of God to make these truths become revelation to you. This is a "Now Word" for the church. It cuts to the core of our very flesh, of our natural desires to do our own thing. Men and women of God must learn submission to a father who truly desires to reveal the father-heart of God.

If we are willing to obey, the future will be marvellous for the body of Christ.

.   —Pastor Jimmy Crompton
          Spiritual father to the author

Contents

Introduction

This book is about you, your destiny, and how to walk into your birthright. It will radically alter your thinking about your place in the body of Christ. It will open a new concept of sonship in your mind. *Where are the sons in the House?* will challenge you to new levels of understanding and revelation as you prepare to be a ***true son in the house*** or alternatively, as a father, raise your sons in your house.

This book will challenge and irritate the independent spirit that so easily attacks many sons, robbing them of God's true destiny and plan for their lives.

I believe the issue of fathers and sons in the body of Christ runs deep within the heart of God. There has been a lot of preaching and teaching to the fathers. Fathers have been educated, exhorted, encouraged, and inspired to take their place as fathers. In recent times it has been revealed how important their function is to raise the young in Jesus to maturity, to father the people of God at great personal cost to themselves. The fathers have tackled this task with enthusiasm, giving their best. They've often been left bewildered and burnt-out after expending themselves in this often thankless work of fathering.

Fathers have also been warned, accused, pressured, and judged for failing in this duty. Many fathers have become hurt and disillusioned as they have lost sons who have rebelled and betrayed them.

In their ignorance, sons have often made the task of fathering impossible. Fathers have been used, abused, and disrespected, struggling in an uphill battle, moved by their conscience and the Holy Spirit to raise up believers into their calling.

Many sons have a one-sided approach to the relationship between fathers and sons in the body of Christ. Their concepts of fathering and sonship are warped and lop-sided. I have seen so many fathers cry tears of sorrow as they have blamed themselves when they have lost wayward sons who have abused and used their father's calling, heart, and commitment.

The purpose of this book is to bring liberty to fathers and sons alike. Fathers will realize that they alone are not responsible for their son's spiritual education. It is a two-way relationship. It takes two hands to clap and two wings to carry an airplane. Sons should also carry responsibility by proactively taking their place in the house.

Sons will learn that it is a great privilege to have a spiritual father. I want to teach the sons to be sons. We must appreciate our spiritual fathers, who are a gift from God. The greatest release into my destiny in God came the day I understood and embraced my responsibility as a son in the house. My decision to be the son that God had called me to be in the house where He placed me released the powerful dynamic that catapulted me into a new dimension of anointing and wisdom that I would never have known any other way.

I have seen fathers cry when they have found release through this message. There has been an awakening in their hearts as they've discovered that all the false guilt and pressure that they've carried, because of disobedient sons, is not theirs to bear.

I've also witnessed many thousands of sons come into true freedom as they've discovered that they don't have to bear the burden of fighting and scratching to defend their destiny.

They've learned how to come to a place of peace and release as they've embraced obedience to God's values that He has taught us in His Word.

As I've taught these principles in churches, I've seen many relationships between fathers and sons become whole. It is a great joy to me to see the local church being restored to her purpose and glory of raising disciples.

Together we will explore the blessings of sonship. I will also expose satan's plans and strategies to steal this glory from your life. I will tell it like it is because I've been there. I know exactly how difficult it can become and how much character it's going to take for you to take your place as a true son in the house. My heart is with you as you read this book. My desire and passion are for you to enter a dimension of satisfaction and blessing that only obedience to God can bring.

Don't just "read" this book. "Experience it." Allow the Holy Spirit to minister new and exciting concepts to your heart. As you prayerfully consider the following chapters, I trust that your life will be forever changed.

Chapter 1

A Multi-Generational God

God does not call a man. **He calls a man and his seed**. He calls a man and the man's seed and the seed of the man's seed and the seed of that seed. Every man of God has the calling to reproduce himself in others. We need to take this seriously. Personally, I've come to realize that, although I may have a clear understanding of what my ministry gifts are, my prime function on this earth is to reproduce myself in others - my spiritual sons. In other words, my first priority is to impart my spirit into others, thereby multiplying the anointing on my life into them.

Unlimited Fruit

To simply live a life of carrying out "my ministry," will result in limited fruit. That would be likened to a tree that just grows big. It will bear some fruit but one day the tree will die. If that tree never reproduces other trees, there will just be a barren landscape left when the tree dies, no matter how big and powerful it became in life.

If you take another tree that reproduces itself, it may or may not grow big, but when it dies, it will leave a whole plantation of other trees that will now reproduce themselves in others because that spirit of impartation has been grafted into them by the parent tree.

This is how the kingdom of God ought to grow. The kingdom of God should be growing in multiplication. This happens when fathers impart their spirit into their sons. Spiritual fathers ought to be like the tree that makes many other trees before it dies. So many people are on a mission to promote their own ministry, gifts, and callings. They're the same as the sapling that grows into a giant tree but never takes the time to reproduce more trees thus leaving only memories of its greatness rather than a living legacy. How many great ministries will come and go leaving behind them only a reputation but no legacy?

Beyond One Generation

God is a multi-generational God. He sees far beyond one generation. We see only our lives, but He sees much further. We live in the now. He *was* before we came. He will be after we leave. In God's mind—in the big plan—our lives occur somewhere in time. He knew our spiritual fathers and their fathers, and will know our spiritual sons and their sons, and so on until the end of time.

God's vision and plan are long term. They are longer than your lifetime and longer than any person's lifetime. Your life-span on earth is but one facet of the vision. God's vision is not only for you. God's vision is for you *and* your sons - just like God's vision was not for your spiritual father only. It was for him and his spiritual sons, including you. His vision is greater than a single generation.

You may be a young man or woman in the Lord as you read this. It will be difficult for you to perceive that the vision that God has for your life includes spiritual sons whom you do not yet have. Believe me, they're on the way! God already knows the individuals whom He wants to send to you for you to father. Therefore, I encourage you to prepare yourself for fathering by being a good son.

I have long understood that my destiny has been vitally entwined in my spiritual father's destiny, just as his destiny was vitally entwined in his spiritual father's destiny. This flow continues as I avail myself as a channel to father others, and that spirit flows to and through my sons to their sons. When you see yourself and your calling in that light, it adds a whole new and fascinating dimension to the relationship between fathers and sons.

So God created man in His own image; in the image of God He created him; male and female He created them (Genesis 1:27-28).

When God created mankind, He saw himself being reproduced in them. He imparted of His own Spirit by breathing the breath of life into that first lifeless body and, in so doing, He imparted His very own nature. God gave that body, which was literally a bag of dust, His own life. He then released the man into his destiny with the next generation of living souls in his loins. God saw beyond the first man. God's vision included the generations to come.

Be fruitful and multiply

Then God blessed them, and God said to them, "Be fruitful and multiply; fill the earth and subdue it; have dominion over the fish of the sea, over the birds of the air, and over every living thing that moves on the earth" (Genesis 1:28).

Adam and Eve were released into their destiny when God spoke the Word over them. Man's destiny was to subdue the earth and have dominion. But first, man was instructed to do something that would be vital in achieving this goal. Man was instructed to *"be fruitful and multiply."*

Today there is a tremendous emphasis on dominion, but I believe that God is reactivating *"being fruitful and multiplying"* in the body, which in turn will result in great dominion. God never intended for the vision to be directed at a single generation only. That's why He instructed Adam to be fruitful. The fruit was to come out of Adam's own loins. Without fruit and multiplication there would be no fulfillment of the vision. The vision was not only for Adam and for those whom he would produce, it was also for those after them and so on.

And the things that you have heard from me among many witnesses, commit these to faithful men who will be able to teach others also (2 Timothy 2:2).

Here, Paul writes to his spiritual son, Timothy, saying the same thing. Observe that there are no less than four generations of believers in this one short verse. Paul writes to his son Timothy to impart to Timothy's spiritual sons who, in turn, will impart to their sons!

As far as I can tell, the last generation mentioned here had not yet been spiritually born. Paul was educating Timothy. He was imparting this very truth—the value of sonship in the body—into his life. This impartation must go from generation to generation to generation until Jesus comes. Sons become fathers, who father sons who become fathers, who will continue the cycle.

This principle is alive today, but is it being embraced in its fullness in the body? God calls and anoints men to fulfill His vision and purpose for God's kingdom on earth. God is saying to these men, "Be fruitful and multiply. Fill the earth with believers and subdue it and have dominion. Fathers, multiply yourselves in your sons. Sons, take your place as sons to your fathers, and walk into your inheritance." Satan would love to short-circuit this process. We must not let him succeed.

It is irrelevant how anointed or how important people become. It doesn't impress me if men and women are honored, have favor, and rise to great ministries. If they do not father others, something's wrong, and they will go home empty-handed. The last thing Jesus did before He ascended to heaven was to impart fatherhood to those who were His sons while He walked on earth as a man.

Take Your Place

Sons, do not reject your spiritual heritage. (I will elaborate on this later.) I can't emphasize this enough! Sons, take your position in the house. Determine today not to give up on your rightful inheritance.

I have three daughters. Jessie-Lee is eleven, Casey is eight, and Jenna is eighteen months. As I watch these three girls grow, I understand that they're at different stages of development. This fact influences the nature of our fellowship. For instance, I have noticed that the younger they are, the more the responsibility of and commitment to our relationship are squarely on my shoulders. This means that I do all the loving, caring, teaching, correcting, protecting, etc. They do all the receiving, demanding, messing, falling, crying, and so on!

However, once children become older, their responsibility in the relationship increases. There comes a stage when children in the house grow to a certain place of maturity that demands that they begin to pursue the relationship in a proactive way by taking their position in the house. At this time the fathers can be doing a great job of fathering, but if the children fail to respond as children in the house, the relationship will not bear as much fruit as it should.

I have found the same principle to be functional in the body of Christ. When the sons in the house fail to take a position that enables them to be effectively fathered, the relationship suffers and often falters. There is a marked difference between men and women who find themselves in a local church as members and those who pursue the attitude and place of sonship.

Those who pursue sonship have a great longing to be one spirit with the shepherd, even to the point of personal sacrifice. They are committed to walk through thick and thin to be faithful sons. They understand that God has joined them to a man of God, and these sons are careful to protect their own hearts. They understand that the success of this unique relationship is as much dependent on them as it is on their father. These are true sons in the house.

No Shortcuts

There are no shortcuts in God's kingdom. I feel sad when I encounter people who desperately want to fulfill their God-given destiny, love Jesus, and be fruitful in their lives, but they find it difficult to submit to God's plan. They struggle to get ahead but seem to only tread water. Even if they do experience some sense of achievement in God's kingdom, it's empty because the foundations are all wrong. I encourage you to open your heart to the dealings of God regarding the spirit of sonship.

Chapter 2
Paul's Son Timothy

For this reason I have sent Timothy to you, who is my beloved and faithful son in the Lord, who will remind you of my ways in Christ, as I teach everywhere in every church (1 Corinthians 4:17).

Appointed Fathers

We understand that God is our Father. We serve God *The* Father. Paul never tried to take God's place in Timothy's life as *The Father*. Rather, Paul was the expression of the fatherheart of God in Timothy's life.

God loves the world, even the worst of sinners. How will they have a revelation of God's love for them? How does God express His love to the world in a tangible way? I'll tell you how - through you and me. God uses His people to demonstrate His love for the world in a practical way on the earth.

How does God exercise authority on the earth? Through His people.

How does God change lives? Through His people.

How does God bind up the broken-hearted and set the captives free? Through His people.

How does God feed His sheep in the church? Through His people.

How does God express His fatherheart and father His people? Through His people whom He has called to fathering.

The Lord has told us that He works by His Spirit and not by might nor by power.

"Not by might nor by power, but by My Spirit," says the LORD of hosts (Zechariah 4:6b).

God works through His Spirit, which flows through His people. The Bible calls the Holy Spirit our helper (paraclete). This helper, whom we know as the Holy Spirit, manifests in many ways in our lives as we avail ourselves as vessels for His purposes.

The Gift of Fathering

There are fathers in the body whom God has raised up to express and exercise His fatherheart. He has placed His fathering spirit in men and women in His church to father others that they, in turn, may grow into good fathers. God fathered Timothy through Paul. Paul was the expression of the fatherheart of God in Timothy's life. Paul was never to take God's *place* as father. Paul was a steward of this gift from God. The ability to father Timothy, by letting the *spirit* of fathering flow from God through Paul to Timothy, was a gift from God.

But now God has set the members, each one of them, in the body just as He pleased (1 Corinthians 12:18).

When God placed me in the body as a spiritual father, I was concerned. I thought that I wouldn't be up to it. I shouldn't have worried. God allowed His fathering spirit to flow through me and into the lives of those whom He had given to me as sons. This has become a fulfilling and rewarding experience for me as I see God father men and women through me. To father men and women for the Lord is a great gift from God. I have come to respect and honor this office and responsibility.

The Gift of Sonship

The spirit of sonship is also manifest in the body of Christ. Just as the fathering spirit flows through the fathers in the house, so the spirit of sonship flows through the sons in the house. This is how Timothy could be called Paul's son. Timothy allowed this spirit of sonship to flow through him, Paul called Timothy, *"my beloved and faithful son in the Lord."* The spirit of sonship was a gift that God had given Timothy.

As a young man, I was given the opportunity to take my place as a son in the house. God had given me a spiritual father, and I was blessed to take my place as a son to him. To see the spirit of sonship flow through my life was a gift that God blessed me with, and I am so grateful that I had the wisdom and courage to embrace this calling.

Timothy himself was also a gift from God. Sons in the house are a special gift from God. Where would I be without my spiritual sons? What blessings they are!

In the same way, Paul was a gift from God to Timothy.

Faithful Son

Paul didn't just call Timothy his son. Paul called Timothy his *faithful* son. What an honor to have your spiritual father call you a *faithful* son. When I came into the house where God had placed me, I became a son. When I embraced the calling as a son, I became a *faithful* son. Many pastors have given so much. They've sacrificed and have laid their lives down to father sons, but often these sons don't understand that they must be sons in order to receive the *benefits* of sonship.

Church members are great, sons are better, and faithful sons are best.

The Fatherless

In my country, we have the phenomenon of street children, especially in the bigger cities. Thousands of children—from as young as three and four years old through young adults—roam the streets. They have no homes. Most choose this life, but others are forced onto the streets through circumstances. They scrounge for money and food and shelter and are open prey to all sorts of dangers and wrong influences. They are fatherless. They have no mentors. They cruise from place to place with no roots anywhere.

A marked characteristic of these homeless children is their incredible lack of discipline. They are also unaccountable, irresponsible, and have no allegiance to anyone. They live for themselves. One day they might act friendly and trustworthy towards a person and the next day proceed to stick a knife in that person without any conscience. It all depends on what's in it for them. This is a sad state of affairs.

Many Christians live a spiritually parallel existence to these homeless people. They go from church to church looking for that which suits them best. Their only interest is seeking what is beneficial to them. They use the local church for their own purposes and don't understand the value of personal sacrifice to bless the body. If something better is happening down the road on any given day, they'll be off without hesitation. These people have no respect for God's ordained authority. They are unaccountable and also unteachable. They do not understand sonship and do not recognize that they should learn from those equipped to mentor them. There is no submission in their hearts. They do not recognize God's divine order and are following their own agenda. They have no real respect for fathers in the Lord. In fact, they consider the local church a vehicle to get them where they want to go and give them what they want in life. In their own minds, they perceive themselves as so important that spiritual leadership should overflow with gratitude that they're there at all!

For all seek their own, not the things which are of Christ Jesus (Philippians 2:21).

I reckon that, even now, some readers are mad at me for writing the previous paragraph. Well, there are more who are rejoicing in what they've just read than those who are not. Those who serve the cause of Jesus Christ with their lives are hungry for the truth. When they find it, they embrace it, even though it may sometimes be tough to endure.

He Proved Himself Faithful

Timothy showed exactly the right spirit. To be a faithful son means just that. *Faithful*. Faithful here is the word *pistos*. It literally means to be *trustworthy and trustful*.

We will only fully discover all about Timothy's deeds when we meet him in heaven one day. However, we can learn much about Timothy and his works in what we read about him in the letters from Paul. We often use Timothy, and the things that Paul taught him, to communicate mighty principles in the church today. There is no doubt that Timothy's influence on the worldwide church throughout time has been awesome.

The remarkable facet of Timothy's make-up that sets him apart, is his ability to embrace the spirit of sonship in his relationship with his spiritual father, Paul.

When Paul said that Timothy was faithful, it was because Timothy had *proved* himself faithful! Paul knew that He could trust Timothy even when his back was turned. He knew that Timothy would lay his life down to get the job done even at the expense of personal sacrifice.

*But I trust in the Lord Jesus to send Timothy to you shortly, that I also may be encouraged when I know your state. For I have no one like-minded, who will sincerely care for your state. For all seek their own, not the things which are of Christ Jesus. But you know his **proven character**, that as a son with his father he served with me in the gospel* (Philippians 2:19-22). (Emphasis added)

The Right Spirit

As a spiritual father, I constantly keep my eye on the sons in my house. I am looking for those t who have Timothy's spirit. By spirit, I mean attitude. Timothy's character had been *proven*. He served with Paul as a father. True sons *serve with* their fathers. In order to take your place in the house, you must come to the place of service *with* your spiritual father.

This is not something that will just fall out of the sky. You must pursue sonship. You must choose to *embrace* sonship. It takes patience as well as perseverance.

Time Will Tell!

A proven character takes time. Your character will only be proven trustworthy over time. Time will produce trials, challenges, and many other situations that will give opportunity for the testing of your character. The testing of your character will expose what's really inside of you. I often say to my people, "It's not about whether you're right or wrong; it's about how you handle each situation in your life."

You can be right about something and use it as an opportunity to allow offence to creep into your heart. You can also be wrong about something and allow offence to creep into your heart.

In other words, God will sometimes put you in a position where your opinion will differ from your father's, and you will also be right. The test is to see how you respond and submit in your heart.

Sometimes I've made a wrong call while my sons have been right. However, because I'm me, I've gone ahead and made a mess anyway. This would be a good opportunity for my sons to get offended, but instead, they pass the test and prove their character.

Let me tell you a story.

Both my wife and I planted and pastor The Garden Route Christian Centre in Knysna, South Africa. As those who have ever planted a church from scratch will testify, there is no textbook on how to do it. We arrived with no money, no home, no church venue, nor any other necessities. We just had to find our way around this task set before us by the Lord. Everything that we'd learned at college about church planting went out of the window. What we experienced, in practice, was a far cry from the theory.

I started preaching in a friend's house. I had no pulpit, the chairs didn't match, and there was no music team or worship leader.

A few people who had joined became part of us and we officially had a church. At the time I thought, "What is wrong with these people? Who would join a setup like this?" I was suspicious because they stayed!

Some are still with us today. One of those ladies is a true son in our house and is working as my personal assistant in our office.

During those formative months, I became very frustrated at the lack of worship ministry in our fledgling church. Early one morning I was praying and complaining to God.

I knew of someone who was available and who also happened to be one of the very best musicians I'd ever met. He was also an accomplished worship leader. However, his lifestyle was out of line. He assumed that my need and his availability automatically set the stage for him to be the worship leader at our church. His assumption was incorrect. I said that I couldn't have him lead the worship until he had proven his character and repented of the issues that were an affront to God's Word. He soon disappeared.

Initially I thought that perhaps I had "blown" the situation. I had made my stand, and it seemed to have cost me dearly. In fact, by this time, I'd turned down no less than three individuals who had stepped forward to take the position as worship leader. I was determined to walk in the values that I believed were correct according to God's Word.

Early one morning, I was praying and complaining to God, saying, "How am I supposed to plant and build this church when there is no worship leader? There's just no one!"

I heard God clearly respond, "Yes, there is someone."

"Who?" I asked. "Who is there?"

God said, "You!"

"Me?!?"

When God speaks the things you don't want to hear, there comes a sinking feeling when you know that the thing you fear has come upon you and there's just no way out. I cannot sing. I cannot play an instrument. I have no rhythm. I cannot keep time. I cannot stay in tune. I cannot keep a melody. I just knew that there was no way out. I was the seed that would have to die before this worship ministry could come to life.

"Die" is a good word here because it describes the way I felt every time I stood in front of the church to lead worship. I would break out in a sweat, and my shirt would be visibly drenched before the preaching started.

I got hold of an old nylon-stringed guitar, one of those that go "chung" as the sound dies at the opening. So it would go chung, chung, chung in different keys to make the music for our worship ministry at Garden Route Christian Centre. I used an old necktie as the guitar strap. What I lacked in ability, I made up for in enthusiasm. I gave it all I had and sang and played with great gusto and zeal.

About four or five months after we started, a young student named Tristan joined us. He was doing his third year practical to complete his college diploma. He was a good musician and very handy with a guitar.

This was the answer to prayer for which I had been waiting. However, I have definite ideas about what I want worship to be in our church. I also believe very strongly in imparting my spirit to my sons, so it wasn't as easy and cut and dried as one would imagine. Tristan had to first prove his character and spend a season with me in this worship ministry before I could let him loose on my flock. He needed time to receive my spirit and anointing. I didn't have the talent or musical skill, but the anointing to lead this flock as father and shepherd rested on me.

This time together proved to be a major challenge and stretching of Tristan's character.

I said, "Follow me." I would launch into praise and worship with great excitement and vigor! There would be the two guitars. I would speed up…and down…speed up…and down, all the time. Me, with my chung, chung and Tristan with his really great-sounding Yamaha. Me, singing out of tune and out of melody and Tristan with his sweet voice holding the notes. He never once complained during those few months. He quietly submitted, although he could have done so much better on his own, and he knew it. He just plodded along and supported me as best he could during those trying times. Often, I would totally lose the church and Tristan as well, and then they would just find their place again and carry on. I was oblivious to all this because I was concentrating so intently.

Tristan proved his character as a true son should in the circumstances. I had other folk come along who just had to be right, and if they couldn't be right and have things their way, they just walked out. Of course, it wasn't a secret that I was hopelessly out of my league leading worship. Tristan was probably bursting inside to take the reigns, but I kept on leading the worship until I was satisfied that he had received enough impartation from my spirit to give him charge of this important ministry. I was also aware that the congregation was wondering just how long I was going to keep on leading worship!

This process paid amazing dividends. Now, six years later, we are known in the area for our praise and worship. We are also in the process of working towards recording our first praise and worship CD with songs written by our team. Today **Pastor** Tristan Deutschmann stands tall as a strong son in my house, and I trust him with my life.

He stood the test. I had to be sure that he had received my heart. I had to find a like-mindedness in him. In the time we were together on the music team I made many wrong calls. He had every reason to rebel and assume a superior attitude, but he didn't. He has proved himself as a faithful son over and over again.

To be Like-Minded

Paul says something important in Philippians 2:20: *"For I have no one **like-minded**, who will sincerely care for your state"* (Emphasis added).

A true son chooses to be like-minded with his father. As a shepherd, it is vital to me that men and women that I raise as sons in the house are going to have the same sincere conviction to love and care for the sheep the way I do. That means that we must be like-minded. With Tristan, it was a case of waiting until he was like-minded and able to lead the worship ministry with the right spirit. Talent and gifting are important, and sons must pursue these with passion. However, first prize is when you flow in the anointing *and* have a like-minded spirit with your spiritual father while exercising your gifts and talents.

For this reason I have sent Timothy to you, who is my beloved and faithful son in the Lord, who will remind you of my ways in Christ, as I teach everywhere in every church (1 Corinthians 4:17).

Here's an interesting statement that Paul makes regarding Timothy. He says that, *"remind you of my ways in Christ."* Have you ever met someone who reminded you of someone else, only to find that they're actually related. That has happened to me. About twenty years ago I was studying a course as part of my secular job before I was in the ministry. The lecturer and his actions looked so familiar. This puzzled me. By the end of the first week I was bursting to the point that my curiosity overcame my embarrassment at asking a stupid question. I had an uncle who lived in a city far away and I hadn't seen or spoken to him for a long time. This lecturer reminded me so much of him.

So I asked, "Excuse me, Sir, do you know a man by the name of so-and-so who's married to so-and-so?"

"Sure," he answered, "he's my brother!"

My amazement was obvious. I didn't even know my faraway uncle *had* a brother!

This is what Paul meant when he said that Timothy would remind them of his ways in Christ. As the fathering spirit flows from the fathers to the sons, the sons receive the father's spirit. There is a clear impartation of the father's heart to the sons.

I never see any evidence of Timothy seeking his own ambition and ministry. I only see how Paul trusts him without wavering. I only see how Timothy's heart is open for Paul to pour in all that he has. I see Timothy, thirsting for Paul's spirit. I know that Paul wasn't a perfect man and there must have been times that it wasn't easy for Timothy, but there is no evidence of Timothy wavering in sonship.

Note that fathering was a strong part of Paul's life. He clearly embraced sonship in his ministry and often encouraged his sons. It was evident that Paul did have other sons.

*I appeal to you for **my son Onesimus**, whom I have begotten while in my chains...*(Philemon 1:10). (Emphasis added)

*To **Titus, a true son** in our common faith: Grace, mercy, and peace from God the Father and the Lord Jesus Christ our Savior* (Titus 1:4). (Emphasis added)

These few are the ones that Paul mentioned. There must have been many more sons in Paul's life. Paul embraced his sons and allowed and encouraged them to flow in sonship because he knew it was God's way of ensuring the multiplying of His church in the generations to come, until Jesus comes to fetch His bride without spot or wrinkle.

Chapter 3

The Altar

I want to relate a specific experience that changed my life forever.

"Get on the Altar, Son"

A number of years ago, I was in a worship service when God's voice penetrated the very depths of my heart. This was a defining moment in my life and I guess the very beginnings of the inspiration behind this book.

The Lord spoke clearly to me, saying, "Son, I want you on the altar."

"Oh yes, Lord." My response was immediate and serious. With all my being I wanted to do the right thing to please God. This is what I live for. I remember I was standing in the front of the church, near the pulpit. The place was thick with the anointing of God. The music was playing, and my pastor was ministering.

God spoke again, "No, son, you don't understand. It's not for me. You're already on the altar for me. You did it when you first got saved and you're still on that altar. I want you on the altar for your spiritual father whom I've placed in your life."

In my heart I could perceive what God was saying. I could even see it, but I couldn't understand it. My mind didn't grab what God was communicating to me. I wrestled with this concept for days. I knew it was God. It just stayed with me. Days became weeks.

I was Frustrated

There were other things I was dealing with. At 30 years of age, dreaming of the ministry, I faced many emotional crises. I was in the local church and felt overlooked. I knew I was called but was getting impatient. There was a tremendous struggle within me and I became restless in my surroundings. I thought I was ready and couldn't understand why I wasn't being released into greater authority. I felt misunderstood and uncared for by my pastor and the leadership. This frustration was beginning to develop into a rebellious seed that was threatening to grow into a fruit-bearing tree. I continually wanted to leave and seek my spiritual fortune elsewhere—somewhere where I'd be more "recognized" and "appreciated." I'd been to Bible College. I understood the dynamics of the ministry, and I could preach the word as competently and powerfully as many of the visiting preachers.

I lived in fear. Fear that I'd be left on the shelf and would have to live in mediocrity because no-one seemed to recognize my gift or the passion for the ministry that burned in my heart. I wasn't entrusted with tasks that I knew I was capable of doing. I was placed in ministry situations that I felt could be handled by less 'mature' folk than me. I felt that I was ready to take on the world. I was given the task of teaching the 'Foundation Course.' I was soon able to teach it without referring to any books. After four years I was so bored with ministering this course every Monday night that I just wanted to break something. Of course, my thinking was way out of line, but I'm painting a picture here to help you realize that you're not the only one experiencing frustration. These are real issues that sons in the house have to face during their walk to spiritual adulthood, and my walk was no different than yours.

I was Harnessed

I thank God for a wise and stable wife. Lynne would often warn me sternly about leaving. Inside of me I always knew she was right. Often I would get really angry, and my frustration would threaten to boil over. Lynne would be there to harness me. Looking back, my irrational instability at that time was evidence enough that I was far from ready to be released.

It was at the height of this trying time that I heard God's voice concerning the altar.

Freedom!

I got the revelation a few weeks after God first spoke to me about being on the altar for my spiritual father. I was reading the Bible one day when I was led to the account in which Abraham obeyed God and took his son Isaac onto a mountain to sacrifice him.

God said that He wanted me on the altar for *my* spiritual father as Isaac had been on the altar for *his* father, Abraham. Suddenly the light shone into the darkness, and my understanding opened. In a flash I could see the picture, and my heart lit up. In this process, I saw deliverance from all of my fears and frustrations. Hallelujah! I knew that I was a free man if I would obey God as He'd shown me! The altar experience is designed to bring release and not bondage, to bring freedom and not chains.

As I read the account of unusual bravery and courage by both father and son, I was filled with admiration. At once I was inspired to learn more and knew that I had stumbled onto a concept so deep and powerful in the heart of God that I just had to get the entire truth.

Then He said, "Take now your son, your only son Isaac, whom you love, and go to the land of Moriah, and offer him there as a burnt offering on one of the mountains of which I shall tell you." So Abraham rose early in the morning and saddled his donkey, and took two of his young men with him, and Isaac his son; and he split the wood for the burnt offering, and arose and went to the place of which God had told him.

Then on the third day Abraham lifted his eyes and saw the place afar off. And Abraham said to his young men, "Stay here with the donkey; the lad and I will go yonder and worship, and we will come back to you."

So Abraham took the wood of the burnt offering and laid it on Isaac his son; and he took the fire in his hand, and a knife, and the two of them went together. But Isaac spoke to Abraham his father and said, "My father!" And he said, "Here I am, my son." Then he said, "Look, the fire and the wood, but where is the lamb for a burnt offering."

And Abraham said, "My son, God will provide for Himself the lamb for a burnt offering." So the two of them went together. Then they came to the place of which God had told him. And Abraham built an altar there and placed the wood in order; and he bound Isaac his son and laid him on the altar, upon the wood. And Abraham stretched out his hand and took the knife to slay his son. But the Angel of the LORD called to him from heaven and said, "Abraham, Abraham!" And he said, "Here I am." And He said, "Do not lay your hand on the lad, or do anything to him; for now I know that you fear God, since you have not withheld your son, your only son, from Me."

Then Abraham lifted his eyes and looked, and there behind him was a ram caught in a thicket by its horns. So Abraham went and took the ram, and offered it up for a burnt offering instead of his son. And Abraham called the name of the place, The-LORD-Will-Provide; as it is said to this day, "In the Mount of The LORD it shall be provided."

Then the Angel of the LORD called to Abraham a second time out of heaven, and said: "By Myself I have sworn, says the LORD, because you have done this thing, and have not withheld your son, your only son— "blessing I will bless you, and multiplying I will multiply your descendants as the stars of the heaven and as the sand which is on the seashore; and your descendants shall possess the gate of their enemies. In your seed all the nations of the earth shall be blessed, because you have obeyed My voice" (Genesis 22:2-18).

When God spoke to Abraham commanding him to take Isaac to the mountain and sacrifice him, He used remarkable words in reference to Isaac. God called Isaac "*your only son.*" This intrigued me, as I well know that Abraham had more than one son. Why would God then say, "your *only* son." As I studied, I found that the original Hebrew word for "only son" used in this scripture is the word *yachid* (pronounced *yahcheed*). This word has its origin in the verb *yachad*, meaning "to be one."

Then He said, "Take now your son, your only son Isaac, whom you love, and go to the land of Moriah, and offer him there as a burnt offering on one of the mountains of which I shall tell you" (verse 2).

As a pastor, I live for fathering the sons whom God has given me. It is my passion to see them develop and grow into God's richest calling and purpose for their lives. To see my sons prosper is my reward and satisfaction. I want them to become more than I will ever be. If I had my way, every member of my church, without exception, would be a *yachid*. However, this does not happen, and there are various reasons for this which I will go into in more detail later. The truth is that only **some** sons can be called *yachid*. These sons stand apart.

Isaac was such a son. He bore the qualities that separated him as *yachid*. I realized that being a biological offspring of Abraham didn't guarantee the status of *yachid*.

Interestingly, the other time a similar phrase appears is when God speaks of **His** *"only begotten Son"*- His *yachid* in John 3:16. Why? Because Jesus was the true demonstration of *yachid*. He was one with His Father as He still is today. Jesus is the absolute representation of the spirit of *yachid*. He understood and responded to the calling to sonship.

Jesus the Son

In the beginning was the Word, and the Word was with God, and the Word was God. ***He*** *was in the beginning with God. All things were made through* ***Him****, and without* ***Him*** *nothing was made that was made* (John 1:1-3). (Emphasis added)

The Word was, the Word was with God, and the Word was God. God is the same yesterday, today, and forever, so the Word still is, still is with God and still is God. The Word is not an "it;" but rather, the Word is "He."

He *was in the beginning with God. All things were made through* ***Him****, and without* ***Him*** *nothing was made that was made* (verses 2, 3). (Emphasis added)

The 'He' and 'Him' refers to a person that we know as Jesus Christ.

I want to help you understand that the concept of sonship was birthed in the heart of God, and He has willed that this value flow through all creation and particularly through His Church.

Consider the Word of God. The Word of God always was. He did not start out in a manger in a stable. Jesus was always there. His life did not begin on earth. He was with God and He was God. He was and is the Word of God. God sent His Word into the earth.

And the Word became flesh and dwelt among us, and we beheld His glory, the glory as of the only begotten of the Father, full of grace and truth (John 1:14).

This Word took on flesh, and He walked the earth as a man. We call Him Jesus Christ.

God says, *"This is My beloved Son, in whom I am well please."* In Matthew 3:17b.

A Special, Special Relationship

God sent the person of His Word into the earth and called this Word His Son. Why would God choose to call the Word that He sent into the earth His Son? Think about it.

God said, "*This is My Son*," so we understand and know that the Word that became flesh and was called Jesus is God's son. Why didn't God call Jesus something else? Maybe "My ambassador" or "My partner" or "My cousin" or one of many other titles that would still have been good? Why *'My Son'*?

God could only call His Word that had been sent to the earth in the flesh His Son because of the powerful factors that constituted this unique interaction between The Father and the Word. No other relational position exists between two parties that adequately embraces the relationship that we see between God the Father and Jesus Christ, the Word become flesh. The extraordinary factors that contribute to this relationship between God and Jesus Christ leave no other choice but to call the Word become flesh God's Son. The very nature and characteristics that constitute this relationship demand that it be described in a way that will adequately communicate the stature it deserves. To call Jesus Christ "The Son of God" tells the whole story of who the Word is in relation to God! To call Jesus Christ something other than God's Son would water down who Jesus is. To call Jesus, who is the Word of God, something else other than the Son of God would weaken our understanding of just who Jesus really is.

So, if you'll bear with me, I'll try and put what I'm saying more plainly.

Before Jesus Christ was born on the earth, God, the Word and the Holy Spirit were in perfect unity. They agreed that mankind's only chance against the power of sin was to send the Word; the Word would become flesh and be born as a man, and He would defeat satan and the power of sin. The Word would go on this mission as 100% man but, at the same time, He would still be 100% God. At this time, the Word was not yet known as The Son of God. This only happened when the Word came into the earth as a man. So, when the Word was manifested in the earth, there was only one concept that adequately measured up to the greatness of the relationship between God and His Word - that is '**Father and Son**.' God then presented Jesus Christ to us as '**the Son of God**.'

There are some very powerful values that exist in this unique relationship between God the Father and God the Son.

For God so loved the world that He gave His only begotten Son, that whoever believes in Him should not perish but have everlasting life. (John 3:16) (Emphasis added)

This phrase, '**only begotten**,' is similar to the phrase '**your son, your only son**.'

*Then He said, "Take now **your son, your only son** Isaac...*(Genesis 22:2). (Emphasis added)

Only begotten, (John 3:16) is actually a title that John accredits to Jesus. It communicates the idea of being *unique*, *special* and *one-of-a-kind*.

Your son, **your only son**, is *yachid*. These two phrases are in different languages—Hebrew and Greek. However, they're saying the same thing.

One is about Isaac in relation to his father, and the other is about Jesus in relation to His Father. Just as we see the traits of true sonship demonstrated in Isaac, so we see the true nature of sonship demonstrated in the life of Jesus Christ.

Both sons laid their lives down so that their fathers' vision might be fulfilled. Both sons, in giving up their lives, possessed their inheritance.

Saying, "Father, if it is Your will, take this cup away from Me; nevertheless not My will, but Yours, be done" (Luke 22:42).

My heart's desire is to see many sons transition from ordinary sons to *yachid*. *Yachid* is one with the father—one in his vision, his purpose, his destiny, and with the father's heart.

My question to you right now is, "What kind of son are you?" "Are you a true son in the house?" "Do you possess the qualities of *yachid*?" As you read this, find out what God is saying to you about your life. Prayerfully consider your place in the house as a son. Those who don't embrace the spirit of *yachid*, struggle. Generally these men and women desire the benefits of sonship but either don't know how to receive them or simply refuse to walk in the values of being a true son in the house.

The spirit of sonship in the body of Christ is neither male nor female. It is not a gender issue.

There is neither Jew nor Greek, there is neither slave nor free, there is neither male nor female; for you are all one in Christ Jesus (Galatians 3:28).

Anyone who has ever gotten close to me will know how much I value and raise up women in our church. I have many 'sons' who are women. As you will see later, this is all about impartation and inheritance. Men and women alike are able to *receive* impartation and destiny as sons, just as men and women alike are able to *give* impartation and destiny as fathers. The reason that sonship is not gender-related is because sonship is *positional*. This means that being a son is not dependent on whether you're male or female, but on how you **position** yourself. So, a woman can enter into the spirit of sonship by **positioning** herself as a son in the body and accepting the responsibilities of a son.

Let me tell you about Felicity. She came to our church a few years ago, brimming with enthusiasm. Everywhere Felicity goes she leaves some influence. You can't spend time with her and not be impacted. Everything about her is expressive. There's a light that shines from her countenance that touches lives. I know her as a person of passion. She says what she thinks, and her outspokenness has often been misunderstood. She's a person of extremes, so when she's up she's really up, and, of course, the opposite also applies. I love her to bits.

When she came to us she wasn't a new Christian. She had been saved for many years. You know what I mean—been there, done that, and got the t-shirt. Now, as any pastor will testify, this can be a great asset or it can be a nightmare.

One day, soon after joining us, Felicity had a speed wobble. It wasn't a big crisis. It was just a little misunderstanding that could have become a huge mess if it wasn't well-handled. I knew from the beginning, that this was inevitable and I was patiently biding my time. I saw it as an opportunity to draw her into sonship.

I called her and began to speak truthfully, directly, and lovingly to her with the attitude of a father. I fathered her and imparted my heart with guidance, counsel, godly wisdom, compassion, and acceptance. Felicity's life changed that day, and she began the transition to the son in the house that God had called her to be. She told me that she had been in some of the biggest ministries in South Africa and had been functioning in the ministry in many aspects but now, for the first time, she had the experience of actually being pastored. No one had ever sat down with her and taken the time to address character issues. She'd always been recognized for the performance that she delivered, and everyone around her assumed that she was all right.

Today Felicity is one of my most trusted sons in my house. I have nicknamed her my "wing-man." I have great respect for her. The unusual thing is that Felicity is about twenty years my senior.

I have learned that it is very workable for fathers to be younger than their sons in the house. At only forty years old, I often have to father people who are older than me. I accept this as a great privilege. I am extremely careful to maintain an attitude of dignity and respect towards those senior in age, giving them the courtesy they deserve. I make it a point to draw on their wisdom and life experience. It is an unusual blessing to find people older than myself who come alongside me in the vision as they position themselves as sons in the house. These sons do not assume that I'm stupid just because I'm younger than they are or that they've been sent by God to help "poor little me." They have come to understand that I'm called and placed, by God, as the father in this house. Their wisdom and life's experience are of great value to me. Boy, are we a great team!

As an aside, as any pastor will testify that when older people join a ministry, they can either be a great blessing or a great pain. If you're in a church in which your pastor is younger than you are, then you must make a decision about sonship. In the spirit, physical age is not an issue. It's the heart condition that counts.

Isaac

As I studied the account of Abraham and Isaac, I found myself seeing things from Isaac's point of view. I sensed the Holy Spirit placing me in Isaac's shoes in order that I may understand and perceive powerful principles of sonship that were manifesting in these difficult circumstances. Right now, I would like you to think about things from Isaac's perspective. Put yourself in his place as we examine how he reacted. Isaac faced the test of his life and passed. Yes, Abraham was being tested, but as we look closer at this remarkable event in history, we will see that Isaac must have gone through a great mental and emotional battle as he submitted to Abraham's word so that Abraham could obey God.

Isaac displayed all the traits of a true son. He demonstrated how to walk as a son and possess his own destiny through obedience in the altar experience. Isaac was *yachid* to Abraham.

Being a Wood-bearer

Consider this. Abraham was an old man; Isaac was a young man. We know how strong and physically developed Isaac must have been because we see that, when they were still afar off from their destination, Abraham placed all the wood for the sacrifice on Isaac, who carried it all the way to the designated mountain in the land of Moriah.

So Abraham took the wood of the burnt offering and laid it on Isaac his son; and he took the fire in his hand, and a knife, and the two of them went together (Genesis 22:6).

If you're going to walk in true sonship, you're going to have to learn to bear loads for your father. Sonship takes an attitude of servanthood and sacrifice. As a father, this is a value that I struggle with. I find it uncomfortable to allow my sons to carry loads for me. However, I am aware of the importance of their character development; therefore, I don't get in the way of what God is doing. I've realized that it's got nothing to do with whether or not I'm capable of carrying things myself. God will cause the sons to carry the load to expose where their hearts are and to teach them values that can only be learned in this way.

Sometimes I find myself getting a mischievous twinkle in my eye when I see the sons in my house struggle under the very loads that I hated carrying in my spiritually formative years. I see these things as God's invention to use up some of that uncontrolled youthful energy!

On a more serious note, though, it is absolutely vital to the kingdom of God that sons take their place as "wood-bearers." Abraham had servants with him, but he didn't order them to carry the wood for the sacrifice. He laid the wood on his son.

There are certain places where only sons can go. If you only knew how deep this goes in the spirit, you would be so ready to embrace sonship in its fullest form. It is a great honor to be a wood-bearer for your spiritual father. I have found that there are certain people I can call on to bear wood for me. I know that I can count on these sons. There is an awesome connection that seems to take place between father and son when the son flexes his muscles and says, "Don't worry, Dad, I've got it." There is something close and intimate about carrying the load for your father. Don't allow the devil to steal this vital part of your life from you. Don't allow what is rightfully your opportunity to be taken from you. Be in the front of the queue to pick up and carry the wood in the house.

I will put loads on my sons that I can easily carry because I'm fathering educating them by stretching them.

By releasing these burdens onto them and allowing the sons to pick up and carry the load, I set in motion a chain reaction of dynamics that causes a strong spiritual flow between us. This releases an impartation of my spirit into my sons. I say *imparting of my spirit* because by being wood-bearers, the sons are activating a powerful dynamic in the spirit realm. This spiritual dynamic is an open door for my heart to flow into theirs as the trust factor grows and deepens. This is a godly pattern. When the sons take up loads for the father, it provides the father opportunity to practically impart teaching to the sons. For instance, I may have a couple in need who are suffering in their marriage. Certainly, I could do the job and meet the need by going to their aid myself. However, if I allow one of my sons to take my place, the opportunity has been provided to give hands-on teaching to my son while meeting the need at the same time. A burden is also taken off of my shoulders.

I find that men and women who will not be wood-bearers do not receive my heart because there is no flow between us.

When the opportunity presents itself, it is important that sons be wood-bearers for their fathers. It goes a million miles toward building and cementing that relationship.

Son's Bread

Jesus said something special in Matthew 15:26: "*It is not good to take the children's bread and throw it to the little dogs.*"

Strangely enough, it is actually the son's "bread" to carry wood for his father. Bread is sustenance. When a son bears loads for his father, it gives him a sense of accomplishment, of belonging, and purpose. This is because he is pleasing to God when he functions as a son in the house. When he pleases God, he's always fulfilled, even when it's hard to do. Son, don't let another receive your bread. Take your place. Carry the wood to your own altar.

Trusting the Fathers

Then He said, "Take now your son, your only son Isaac, whom you love, and go to the land of Moriah, and offer him there as a burnt offering on one of the mountains of which I shall tell you" (Genesis 22:2).

God spoke only to Abraham. God didn't say, "Now listen Isaac, I'm going to test your daddy to see if he'll obey me in all things and to see if he loves me above all else. Don't you worry now, it's all under control and I'll not let anything happen to you. Just you relax and rest in me. It's your daddy who is being tested."

Nope, God didn't breathe a word to Isaac about anything. Isaac had nothing to trust in except the word of his father.

You see, one of the principles of sonship is that sons must come to the place of trust where they recognize that God gives direction and vision for the house to the fathers and not to the sons. Sons follow the fathers and not the other way round.

Out of Divine Order

Sons fall out of divine order when they attempt to direct the vision for the house. As a son in the house, you will invoke the blessing of God on your life by assuming the same attitude as Isaac and following the vision of your spiritual father, even when it's not comfortable or doesn't make sense to you.

The Word of Authority Under Attack

Satan will always try and wriggle 'himslimyself' between you and your father in the Lord. The way he does this is by attacking the credibility of the father's word. He wants to create a question in your mind regarding your father's word and integrity and his ability to hear God. Satan will always try and destroy the credibility of *all* spiritual authority.

This is how he first did it and this is how he will always do it.

God Instructed Adam

And the LORD God commanded the man, saying, "Of every tree of the garden you may freely eat; but of the tree of the knowledge of good and evil you shall not eat, for in the day that you eat of it you shall surely die." And the LORD God said, "It is not good that man should be alone; I will make him a helper comparable to him" (Genesis 2:16-18).

When God gave the instruction to man about not eating of the fruit of the knowledge of good and evil, He did not speak to Eve, He spoke to Adam. It was Adam's job to tell Eve what God had said. Eve had not yet been created from Adam's rib when God gave the instruction!

God did not Instruct Eve

Eve had never heard God speak of this fruit that she was not to eat. All she knew is what *Adam* told her about what God had said. She had to trust in Adam's word, which she had to assume was correct. Everything was going well until this point. We don't know how much time had passed since Adam told Eve what God had said, and in all that time, while God's divine order was in place, there was peace in the garden.

Broken Trust

So when satan came slithering along he had one goal—to bring an element of mistrust in Eve's heart. This mistrust was directed at *Adam's* word, not God's. Adam was the delegated authority. If satan could cause a breakdown of trust between Adam and Eve, he had a good chance of victory over them.

Now the serpent was more cunning than any beast of the field which the LORD God had made. And he said to the woman, "Has God indeed said, 'You shall not eat of every tree of the garden'?" (Genesis 3:1)

So how did satan get an opening into Eve's heart? He placed a question mark in her heart about Adam! Satan was in effect saying, "Eve, are you sure that Adam heard God correctly? Maybe Adam misinterpreted what the Lord was saying? Perhaps God said something else and Adam informed you incorrectly. After all, he isn't God!"

For God knows that in the day you eat of it your eyes will be opened, and you will be like God, knowing good and evil (Genesis 3:5-6a).

"You see Eve, Adam's got it wrong, you won't die if you eat of the fruit. Adam's mistaken. Anyway, why would God not want you to eat of this fruit if it's going to bless you with the knowledge of good and evil? Uh-uh, I don't think God said it quite like that."

This opened the door just enough for her to start examining the fruit more closely. Big mistake!

So when the woman saw that the tree was good for food, that it was pleasant to the eyes, and a tree desirable to make one wise, she took of its fruit and ate (verse 6a).

Now Eve was looking at the fruit from a different perspective, that of "What if Adam's wrong? He could be, you know. The tree looks good, the fruit looks good, and besides, what's wrong with being wise? I think the snake's right."

"Gotcha!"

In Adam and Eve's relationship, Adam was the delegated authority. The Lord delegates from above; satan attacks from below.

"So Son, Did God Really Say…?"

Getting back to Isaac. Satan was probably whispering in his ear, "Isaac, you know this is wrong. Why are you going along with this? Are you nuts! Listen Isaac, if you get on that altar you're dead meat, man! You'll never see the sun come up again. Do you know what that means? It means that if you hang around here with this guy any longer, he's going to destroy your calling. Isaac, open your eyes! You're being used. Do you think your father even cares about you? He doesn't care. If he did, he'd never expect you to do such a thing! He'd want you to be blessed, but instead he's giving you a hard time. He's only thinking of himself and *his* calling."

"Isaac, did you know that this is unscriptural? So how can this be from God? All this human sacrifice and all? You should challenge your father head-on and put him in his place for getting out of line. You know how called and set apart you are; it's time to make a stand. It's time to make your move before this man messes it all up. ***Did God really say…?***"

Pressure

Surely Isaac had to deal with these issues in his heart. He must have been under immense pressure. I'm sure that his heart was pounding and that he could hear his own breath in his head. Perhaps he sensed claustrophobia and fear, breaking out in a sweat at the thought of, "I'm it! I'm the sacrifice!" But because Isaac was Abraham's *yachid*, he made the correct choice to submit to the altar and to his father's word.

Much of the present day thinking in the local church would have resulted in Isaac forfeiting his destiny at the expense of the lost value of sonship in the house. In fact, if, hypothetically speaking, Isaac were able to travel in time and come to the modern church for counseling regarding his choice, he would more than likely have been told that Abraham was from the devil and that Isaac must cut loose from him.

Have you had similar ideas pop into your head? Dearest sons, be *so* careful to guard the door of your heart.

What God has Joined Together

Therefore what God has joined together, let not man separate (Matthew 19:6b).

Yes, I am aware that Jesus was referring to marriage in this reference, but my argument is that this principle remains constant in any God-inspired, covenant relationship. Jesus often taught us principles rather than rules. "*What God has joined together, let not man separate,*" is one of these principles or values that flows through all of life and is not only in reference to marriage.

So, Where's the Lamb?

When they get to where Abraham builds the altar, Isaac is already wary of something unusual unfolding. He asks his father where the lamb is for the burnt offering and receives a somewhat unusual answer.

And Abraham said, "My son, God will provide for Himself the lamb for a burnt offering." So the two of them went together (Genesis 22:8).

God is Faithful

I would like to address all the sons with a word of encouragement. God will never require more of you than you can bear. Your destiny is in His hands and He will see to it that it comes to pass. Just be faithful as a son. God will see you through. If you are obedient, God will cause your destiny to come to pass. No man, organization, government, or anything else, past, present, or future will be able to rob you of your calling.

As a young man I believed that the calling of God rested on my life, but my biggest fear was that I would disappear into the woodwork and not fulfill my calling. When I was called to the "Isaac altar," I had to face this fear head-on and deal with it once and for all! I came into the place of freedom when I received the revelation that God will complete in me the work that He had started, despite my human weakness and that of men around me.

Be Careful

Here is a word of caution. Many people get this revelation and actually use it to excuse their rebellion or independence. "Well, I just don't need anyone anymore because God is on my side" or "I got a prophecy from God and now no matter what I do, it'll come to pass" or "There's a calling on my life. The anointing will guarantee my destiny." Unfortunately they have a rude awakening on the way. All of God's promises are conditional. Even God's promise to Abraham was conditional on his obedience regarding giving up Isaac and on Isaac's obedience regarding giving his life on the altar.

God has not given you vision and promise that guarantee you success no matter how you behave. You can quite easily scuttle that destiny through disobedience. God has given you vision and promise to see you through personal sacrifice so that you'll stand despite mountains and valleys. He's given you vision and promise to keep you focused when you're tempted to leave the path. You have vision and promise from God to contradict adverse reports and unbelief. Vision and promise from God should be alive in your heart to give you the confidence and trust that you need to submit yourself to biblical principles of accountability, discipline, and mentoring.

Being confident of this very thing, that He who has begun a good work in you will complete it until the day of Jesus Christ (Philippians 1:6).

As a young man I became increasingly aware of the fact that the devil was going to throw all that he could at me to knock me off the track that God had set before me. I decided that no matter what I had to go through, it would be OK! God would see to it that I made it. I had already determined that the achievement of the goals set before me was inevitable because He would see to it that that which He had begun in me, He would complete. It became a lot easier for me to have this confidence when I submitted my heart and will to obey Him as I sought to take my place in the house as a son.

When Abraham said to Isaac, "*My son, God will provide for Himself the lamb for a burnt offering,*" the message was that there is peace in submission. This peace comes when you understand that it's not the SACRIFICE that God demands but the obedient and sacrificed HEART!

Choice

So now try and picture this. Abraham is an old man,well over 100 years old. Isaac is a strong, young man. Somehow Isaac has to get on that altar. This will happen in one of two ways, by force or choice.

I remember an incident, years ago, when I was still dating my wife. It was a hot summer's afternoon and the two of us were goofing around in a swimming pool. We were laughing and splashing and having extravagant fun together. Suddenly she caught me off-guard and grabbed my head and pushed me under the water. Well, this meant war! I went for her quickly. I wanted to give her a good dunking. I guess it had a lot to do with my dented ego that needed fixing. (It's a man thing. I'm a man. I've got feelings). Anyway, I got a hold of her after a chase. Now, my wife is not a big woman. I am a lot larger and stronger than she. I found that pushing her head under the water was not as easy as I thought it would be. Just getting a hold of her was very difficult.

Have you ever tried to dunk someone who doesn't want to be dunked? It's not easy!

Think of Abraham trying to get Isaac onto the altar if Isaac didn't want to be there.

Then they came to the place of which God had told him. And Abraham built an altar there and placed the wood in order; and he bound Isaac his son and laid him on the altar, upon the wood (Genesis 22:9).

When they reached the place that God had pointed out, Abraham first arranged the wood and then had to bind Isaac. Have you ever tried to tie someone up when they don't want you to, especially if that person were a lot younger and stronger than you? I am convinced that Isaac would have had to have submitted willingly for Abraham to bind him.

Abraham lay Isaac on the altar. Once again, the same issues are relevant. Abraham could only have placed Isaac on the altar with Isaac's complete cooperation. The Bible isn't clear whether Isaac climbed onto the altar himself, whether Abraham tied Isaac's feet later or not at all, or whether Abraham was able to pick Isaac up and physically place him onto the altar. Regardless, Isaac had to have complied completely. He *chose* to do exactly as his father desired.

It would be a problem, if not impossible, for the *older man*, Abraham, to get the *younger man*, Isaac, onto the altar if Isaac didn't want to be on that altar! Imagine Abraham trying to bind Isaac and force him onto the altar and Isaac fighting all the way. I do not believe that Abraham had the strength to physically force him against his will.

Can you imagine atypical son's reaction to the suggestion that he should lay on an altar to be slaughtered as a human sacrifice merely at his father's word?

"Now, hold on, Dad. You can't be serious? What do you mean, 'on the altar?' You want me to lie still so that you can tie me up and stick that long knife in my chest and set fire to all this wood under me? Really?"

The Power of Choice

I must conclude that Isaac came to be on the altar by *choice*. His own choice. It was his choice to lay down his life. Isaac had to humbly submit himself. He literally had to come like a sheep to the slaughter.

The true son, the *yachid*, lays down his own life so that the father's vision can come to pass. The true son lays his own life down so that the father can walk in obedience to God and fulfill his calling.

It is that heart of the *yachid* that says, "I will put my own ministry aside for this time. I will serve my father with obedience and commit my life to see *his* destiny fulfilled." Someone once said that you will not see your own vision come to pass until you help someone else fulfill theirs.

What would Abraham have done if Isaac refused to submit? Refused to have his hands tied? Refused to cooperate? There is no way, physically, that Abraham would have been able to force Isaac onto the altar. Abraham depended on Isaac. He also knew Isaac's heart of obedience. In fact, I don't think it even entered Abraham's thinking that he might have a problem getting his son onto the altar. Isaac's absolute obedience was assumed. This was because Isaac was Abraham's *yachid*.

When God first spoke to me about sonship in the house, He made something very clear to me. He said, **"The vision of fathers is built on the lives of the sons who have been laid on the altar."**

This sounds kind of radical, but I know God to be that way. When I began to think about it, it made a lot of sense to me. Abraham's vision was dependent on His son's obedience. Abraham's calling was literally built on Isaac's life on the altar. Personally, I was uncomfortable with this idea when sons were added to me by the Lord. It was difficult for me to accept that my destiny and vision was being built on the lives of the sons in my house! I guess that my embracing sonship in my earlier years made it easier for me to respond to this important value in God's kingdom and has bred a great deal of respect and responsibility in my heart toward these sons.

Redefining Yourself

The role of the sons is vital. If you're struggling to find yourself and your identity in the house that you're in, it is time to redefine who you are.

Are you just a church member? Redefine yourself to become something more.

Are you only on the edge of things, hanging around the perimeter of the body? Come into the center and take your place as a true son.

Are you inside but dissatisfied and critical? Renew your mind, rip out the root of bitterness, join your heart to the heart of your leader, and become a son.

Are you in the body but just an observer and not a participator? Change your heart and commit to begin to function proactively in the house as a son should.

Redefine yourself.

Dying to Everything

And Abraham stretched out his hand and took the knife to slay his son (Genesis 22:10).

This was the moment of truth. It was also the moment that Isaac would die. There was an incredible sacrifice that Isaac was laying down at that altar. His entire destiny was at stake!

There is no record that God had actually spoken to Isaac about his destiny prior to this day. Isaac was in line to inherit Abraham's calling. While God may not yet have spoken to Isaac about it, His father surely would have.

Abraham would have sat with young Isaac under the desert sky when Isaac was a small boy, Perhaps he would have said, "You know little guy, you see all those stars out there? Try and count them."

One, two, three…four hundred and fifty-seven, four hundred and fifty-eight…oh no, I'm mixed up Dad. I can't count them! There are too many. It's impossible to count all of those stars, Dad!"

"Ok, son, you don't have to count them all. I'm just trying to show you what God showed me. You see, all those stars are too many to count, just like the generations coming after us. God made me a promise that we would be a blessing to all the nations of the world, and like all the stars, our descendants would be too many to number."

"Son, you're the beginning of that blessing. Through you, the promise that God made to me will be fulfilled."

So Isaac began to learn from His father about the covenant promise of God and how he was vitally involved. Now Isaac faced death. What about his destiny? His calling? All that his father told him about this wonderful God and all the promises He had made? Isaac would have been tempted to think of his father as a liar, "What about the stars? What about all that you told me? Why get me so excited and looking forward to the day when I step into my inheritance, just to have me come and die on this altar?"

I've seen disappointment on the faces of my children. This is how it works. Monday afternoons are for Jessie. We do fun things together, just the two of us. Tuesdays are my day off. I switch off all telephones, and it's just Lynne and me. No ministry or emergencies are allowed. Friday afternoons are Casey's time. She and I do things together. Now, because of the ministry, it's inevitable that there are times when I have to go out of town or some other thing comes up that I really, really can't avoid. When this happens I have to break the news to the girls, and it pains me to see the disappointment of a broken expectation.

Think of what Isaac faced.

Raising the Dead

You know, even though Abraham was being severely tested here, he still had a deep sense of conviction that God would spare Isaac. He knew that, somehow, Isaac was going to live.

And Abraham said to his young men, "Stay here with the donkey; the lad and I will go yonder and worship, and we will come back to you" (Genesis 22:5).

Abraham said, "We will come back to you." He didn't say, "*I* will come back to you."

He said, "*We* will come back to you." Everything that Isaac did at this time was with trust in the word of his father.

Furthermore, the Bible tells us in Hebrews:

By faith Abraham, when he was tested, offered up Isaac, and he who had received the promises offered up his only begotten son, of whom it was said, "In Isaac your seed shall be called," concluding that God was able to raise him up, even from the dead, from which he also received him in a figurative sense (Hebrews 11:17-19).

Let me assure you, sons in the house, God is in the business of raising the dead. Abraham knew it. What God had promised would come to pass. As a spiritual father over sons, I have to believe, like Abraham, that when I see my sons lay their destinies down on the altar, we're both coming down from that mountain. I must believe that my legacy and spirit will be carried forward into the next generation, as I am carrying my spiritual father's legacy and spirit into the nations. I see the sons literally die before me. I know that God will raise them from the dead and bring their calling to life when the time is right.

Have Understanding

Sons, please understand what is happening when it seems that your father is uncaring and selfish by sacrificing you on that altar. This is the pattern and plan in the kingdom. God requires the fathers to lay their sons on the altar. As the sons rise from their altars they come forth as tried by fire and inherit God's awesome promise that he made to their fathers. Every generation takes up their position on the altar for the previous generation. This ensures that the church multiplies in power and authority.

I understand that it can be frustrating for you when you see the unfaithful and lazy sons having it easy. You may be tempted to ask the question, "Why me? It seems that I'm always the one who carries the wood and takes up the load for my spiritual father in the house. What about the other guys?" Well, that's just the point! You will only find those sons who can be called yachid on that altar. You will look back years from now, when you've completed the cycle and you are flowing in the calling and destiny that God has for you, and you will see these other sons way behind and fruitless. You will then comprehend why it was necessary for you to take the high road.

As I look back over the years and see the lives of my generation and how far they've come with God, I see very obvious differences between us. I'm talking about men and women whom I have known intimately for many years. Many of these folk have lost their inheritance. They seem empty and unfulfilled. Yes, they're saved, but they are bearing no fruit. All the dreams that we shared as young people have been lost somewhere along the way. I'm shocked at their lack of spiritual foundation. Some of these people were my *seniors* in the church that I attended. Now I see only weakness and waste. This is why I'm so passionate about sonship in the house. I want to prevent this from happening. So many lost destinies!

I was the guy in our church that wasn't expected to go far. I was the one who was supposed to be unfruitful and a failure. I started out with ten bricks stacked against me, but because I embraced the altar, God has taken me to the other side.

I remember my youth pastor. He was called of God and anointed. I attended the youth ministry, and I looked up to him and saw him as a role model. With all his talents and gifts, he was unable to bring himself to the Isaac altar. He got involved with some rebellious people who claimed a prophetic ministry. This was a big mistake. Because he was a son with an agenda, which opposed the Isaac altar, he was an open target for satan. So these people began to give him all sorts of "prophetic words: to encourage him because he was having such a "hard time" with our spiritual father. The writing was on the wall. The youth ministry began to fall apart. One day when the senior pastor was on holiday, this young man casually phoned and resigned. This caused major problems in the church, and the senior pastor had to cut his vacation short to come and sort out the mess.

This young man married a woman despite the senior pastor's warnings against it. He married her because those rebellious folk gave them a prophecy that they should be married. Today, about fifteen years later, he's been divorced and remarried. I believe that he has missed God's best. Sure, he might have some success, but whatever he achieves in this life, he will never rise to the destiny that God had intended for him.

Big Decisions

I believe that there are some decisions from which people never recover. The consequences are so damaging that they cost a lifetime to repair. Think very carefully before you react to things. People often live in a false security that says they can do whatever they like and fix it later. Many choices have such devastating fallout that it affects them all their lives.

Isaac was Abraham's *yachid*. Isaac, therefore, laid down all those issues—his destiny, his vision, and his calling. He was even prepared to lay down the very promise that was his inheritance.

When he lay on the altar, all those things lay there as well.

"My Ministry"

A question that sons frequently ask is, "What is my ministry?"

I remember asking that question after my salvation in 1982. When I came into Christian circles and began fellowshipping in the church with Christian guys and girls of my own age, I realized that everyone had a ministry. They were either already in their ministry or going to go into their ministry, but there was always a ministry. So I began the quest to discover my ministry.

This journey took me to weird and wonderful places. I had to find my ministry.

I turned to prophecy and ran after every prophetic ministry that came along. I listened to everyone's wise opinion and did all I could to find it. My heart was hungry for my ministry. It was as though my very success as a Christian depended on me having a ministry. Eventually I "discovered" it. My ministry was that of an evangelist! I found great significance in this knowledge. It seemed as if I'd arrived and that now I was really part of the team. (This was not so. My life and ministry would turn out quite differently).

When God challenged me to lay my life on that altar, the greatest problem that I had was laying down the ministry calling. All of my destiny, significance, value, and future lay in the ministry that I had. More accurately, my ministry!

Two of the most destructive words in the church today are "my ministry!" People have split churches over "their ministry." They've fought, argued, defended, wrestled, become ugly, entertained fruits of darkness, become bitter, and attacked brothers and spiritual fathers, all for the cause of "their ministry." Let me clarify what I mean. It's the same thing as the most misquoted scripture in the Bible, which reads:

For the love of money is a root of all kinds of evil, for which some have strayed from the faith in their greediness, and pierced themselves through with many sorrows (1 Timothy 6:10).

Most people say this:

Money is a root of all kinds of evil, for which some have strayed from the faith in their greediness, and pierced themselves through with many sorrows.

Money is not a root of evil, but the *love* of money is.

In the same way, my ministry is not the problem. It's the love of my ministry! It is obsession that dictates a person's values and reactions in life. Some people live as if their ministry is the breath of life itself. Have you ever seen how someone panics when they get into a situation in which their air supply is inhibited? They will become frantic in order to get that next gasp of air into their lungs. If you happen to get in the way, you'll be in trouble because that person is out of control. This happens when people feel so obsessive about their ministry. They will attack and deal with anyone and anything that threatens their ministry.

To be a true son in the house, you must lose the *love* of *your ministry*, whatever that may be. As Isaac laid his life on the altar, so should you. This is a very difficult thing to do. It is a great test of will and character to make this decision. I struggled with this part.

God expected me to lay down all that I lived for. If someone made me an offer that ensured a peaceful life on earth with no worries but with no ministry, I'd choose to go home to be with Jesus, thank you very much. I felt there was no point in being alive if my ministry was taken away from me. Surrendering to the altar caused a great dilemma for me because I had to lose the all consuming love for my ministry.

In order to help my spiritual father fulfill his calling, I had to come to the point of actually committing my heart to laying my ministry down. This was agonizing to my soul. It felt as though my insides were being ripped apart, but I knew I had to do it.

Satan's Threat

The reason why the words "my ministry" are such a powerful weapon in satan's hands is because he has managed to entrap so many sons in the lie that they have to fight and scratch with all their power to protect their ministry. If you love your ministry to the point that you get fearful at the thought of losing it, then you're an open target for satan's schemes, and you're on dangerous ground. God requires you to lay it on the altar so you can come to a place where satan has no access to your life in this area. He must not be allowed to be in a position where he can manipulate you through fear and unbelief relating to your calling. You must never position yourself where satan can threaten you by saying, "Well, if you don't do what I want, I'll take your ministry!" or, "If you do that, it will cost you your ministry!"

Peace & Freedom

In the church in which I grew up, I personally saw many anointed and called sons lose everything as they fought so hard to protect their ministry. (I spent fifteen years in one church as a faithful son. In that time I never once strayed away or visited another church out of anger). As I placed myself, including my ministry on that altar, I entered a realm of peace and freedom in the ministry. On the altar I could lay back, relax in the spirit, and allow God to do what he had to do in order to take me on to my destiny.

Yes, as I surrendered and placed myself to support my father's vision, I was tempted to feel vulnerable and open to abuse. This is a reality that all sons must face. Questions flooded my mind.

"What if I get stuck here in this church and grow old and go no further in the ministry?"

"What if I never get recognized for what I believe I am called to?"

"What if I am simply kept here and used for my abilities?"

Many more questions assailed my mind. However, I learned to immediately counter these thoughts with the real peace in my heart that came with obedience.

God is building His church. He is not about to be divided against himself. As long as you're obedient, He is going to see to it that you have victory. It is God's will to win. I'll say it again: it is God's will to win. In fact, God is winning and will *continue* winning. It's better to be on his side working with Him; working with Him to win!

God Will Provide a Way

But the Angel of the LORD called to him from heaven and said, "Abraham, Abraham!" So he said, "Here I am." And He said, "Do not lay your hand on the lad, or do anything to him; for now I know that you fear God, since you have not withheld your son, your only son, from Me." Then Abraham lifted his eyes and looked, and there behind him was a ram caught in a thicket by its horns. So Abraham went and took the ram, and offered it up for a burnt offering instead of his son. And Abraham called the name of the place, The-LORD-Will-Provide; as it is said to this day, "In the Mount of the LORD it shall be provided" (Genesis 22:11-14).

God will protect you. He will not let any harm come to you. No matter how heavy the load is as a wood-bearing son or how final the altar seems, God will not let you down. Remember, it's not the sacrifice that he desires, it's your **heart**.

No temptation has overtaken you except such as is common to man; but God is faithful, who will not allow you to be tempted beyond what you are able, but with the temptation will also make the way of escape, that you may be able to bear it (1 Corinthians 10:13).

The word for "tempted" speaks of testing, where one is scrutinized and examined. God says two things very clearly:

First, you will never be tested beyond your ability to pass the test. This means that everything that God ever puts before you, you will be able to endure and accomplish, including the Isaac altar.

Second, with the testing, God will always provide a way of escape for you. This promise is a tremendous source of consolation and a reason to be confident in the middle of a trial. Once you learn to put your trust in God's unfailing character, you'll be far less intimidated by the sometimes seemingly impossible requirements of Christian living. Do not be mistaken. It is by no means an easy road, but it is a certain road to your destiny.

I'd like to add a short note at this time. This is to help sons understand that fathers also go through a great deal of testing. I, as a father, have had to take many sons to the altar. The painful part for me is not knowing how the sons will respond. I can do my part, even at great cost, but if sons do not respond, then I know that I've lost them as *yachid*. This may sound simplistic, but actually, I'm experiencing great emotion even as I write this.

Think about how Abraham must have felt. He had no guarantee that Isaac was going to respond in obedience. I'm sure that he knew his son Isaac and was confident that Isaac's character would "hold out," but there must have been the question in Abraham's mind, "What if Isaac won't do this?"

I've had some sons whom I've loved and enjoyed, sons with great gifting for whom I have laid my life down, but who were not able to face the Isaac altar. I have gone through great pain, sadness, and disappointment as I have obeyed God and taken them to the altar, only to lose them as their character failed them. They are overcome by the fear that, once they are on the altar, they'll never rise again. They cannot bring themselves to trust God's promise that He will never test them beyond what they can bear and that, with the testing, he will **always** provide a way of escape. I believe that by now, the revelation is sinking in. You could still be wrestling with this issue or perhaps be embracing it with great excitement.

Chapter 4

Surrendering The Inheritance

Now Jacob cooked a stew; and Esau came in from the field, and he was weary. And Esau said to Jacob, "Please feed me with that same red stew, for I am weary." Therefore his name was called Edom. But Jacob said, "Sell me your birthright as of this day." And Esau said, "Look, I am about to die; so what is this birthright to me?" Then Jacob said, "Swear to me as of this day." So he swore to him, and sold his birthright to Jacob. And Jacob gave Esau bread and stew of lentils; then he ate and drank, arose, and went his way. Thus Esau despised his birthright (Genesis 25:29-34).

This account of Esau and Jacob has always served as a stark warning to me. It has made me all too aware of the devil's schemes to seduce me and offer alternatives to my destiny in God. There have been many opportunities to take up the devil's offers, which are always candy-coated with false promises and easy ways out of tough times. I have respect for God's calling and I know that the fulfilling of my destiny is not a guarantee. It's dependent on my obedience and on having a steadfast attitude toward the calling of God on my life. I find that so many people place cheap value on obedience and therefore on their calling. They entertain a false notion that, no matter what they do, their calling is inevitable. This is not true. I want to encourage the sons in the house to begin to develop a great, holy respect for their calling and to therefore, be very, very cautious about making rash decisions that serve to satisfy the flesh in the heat of the moment. Nurture your calling. Treat your calling with awe and responsibility. Fear God. Your calling is holy. This means that it ought to be consecrated to God. It should not be taken lightly nor is it a toy for you or anyone else to play with.

A Holy Calling

Don't be under the illusion that "no matter what I do, my calling will come to pass anyway." If you mess it up, it won't happen.

Who has saved us and called us with a holy calling, not according to our works, but according to His own purpose and grace which was given to us in Christ Jesus before time began (2 Timothy 1:9). (Emphasis added).

I'm not suggesting that you must act in the flesh and allow yourself to be filled with anger and bitterness in order to hold onto your calling. I'm saying that you must protect your calling by being obedient to God in all things, especially when you're under great pressure and it seems that your very survival is at stake. Walk in obedience in your relationship with your spiritual father and in your relationship with the people around you in the house. Be in obedience to the word that we have been given by God. Honor the house where you've been placed.

Consider the following:

Weary Esau

Now Jacob cooked a stew; and Esau came in from the field, and he was weary (Genesis 25:29).

Esau came back from a hunt.

The Bible often uses language that is fairly straightforward and seems somewhat underpowered. Here the word "weary" is a typical example. Let me explain just what "weary" speaks of in this instance.

"Weary" means very, very tired. "Weary" means that he was so fatigued that he was just about crawling into that tent. Esau had come back from a hunting trip empty-handed. He had not eaten for days. He was utterly spent. He was very hungry. His body would have been sore and weak from rough traveling on foot with nothing to eat for a long time.

Nowadays, if one goes hunting, he or she may go to a farm with wildlife and take a shot with a high-powered rifle from a very long range, aiming through a telescopic sight. There is a truck available, and the hunter can merely drive up to the carcass and winch it onto the back. Then the carcass is delivered by the truck to a processing plant where it is skinned, and the meat is cut and bagged for the shooter. The taxidermist prepares his trophy for him in a short while.

Hunting was different then.

Esau came home hungry and tired. He would have gone hunting for days. His weapons would have been primitive, and the very nature of the hunt would have been backbreaking work. He would have to get close up to the animal because his weapons couldn't hit the game from afar off. After stalking and tracking his prey on foot for long distances, Esau would have to get close enough for the shot or throw. Once he hit it, it wouldn't be an instant kill. He would be forced to track the animal until it died. So, even hitting the prey didn't mean that he was actually going to *bag* the prey. We know that he came back empty-handed, so he must have spent a very long time wandering around in vain.

The point that I'm making here is that his physical and mental need was extreme. He was at an all-time low. At that moment, the pressure on Esau would have been overpowering. His flesh would have been screaming at him for relief, and he was on a quest to meet those needs.

He Failed

Esau was also under tremendous emotional and psychological strain. To Esau and the rest of the family, a successful hunt was a foregone conclusion, but this time it didn't happen. So he must have also been experiencing an emotional downer. He felt like a failure for coming back empty-handed. He was a man of the land. This meant that he found his significance and identity through providing for his family by hunting and bringing home sustenance. It would make him proud to come home with the proof of his success hanging over his shoulder. This time, though, there was nothing. It was his job in the house, and he had failed. He would have been experiencing disappointment and even anger that his area of authority and expertise had been undermined by his own malfunction as a hunter.

Yes, he was weary in every sense of the word, physically and emotionally.

All Sons Will Become Weary

Sons in the house, on the authority of God's Word and the experience that life has offered me, I assure you that you are going to find yourself in exactly the same situation as Esau did, many times over. As you grow in the house, your toil and work are going to bring you to the place where, at times, you're going to feel just as fatigued as Esau, emotionally and physically. You will become weary. The days will come when you will be so pressurized that everything inside of you will cry out for you to make the easy, wrong choices.

And Esau said to Jacob, "Please feed me with that same red stew, for I am weary." Therefore his name was called Edom (Genesis 25:30).

Esau's hunger was the only thing on his mind when he came home. The pangs in his stomach would not let him go. It was a need that had to be met. He expressed that need very clearly to Jacob who was cooking a stew. The good smell wafted across his nostrils, and his mouth watered. His body cried out for food. He was at the point of desperation.

Sell Me Your Birthright

But Jacob said, "Sell me your birthright as of this day" (Genesis 25:31).

Jacob saw a gap and pounced. Jacob made Esau a straight offer. In essence he was saying, "I have the ability to meet your immediate physical need and take away the all-consuming pain of the hunger that envelops you. There is a price though - I want your inheritance! If you give that to me, I can make all this hardship go away. I can make you feel good, right now. It's yours, but it's going to cost you."

Esau Lost Control

Accumulatively, these inward and outward struggles weakened Esau's resolve and caused him to lose control. Esau became reactive. 'Reactive' means that the circumstances moved him, not that he moved the circumstances. He became a ship without a rudder, steered predictably to and fro by the wind and waves of his circumstances.

And Esau said to Jacob, "Look, I am about to die; so what is this birthright to me?" Then Jacob said, "Swear to me as of this day." So he swore to him, and sold his birthright to Jacob (Genesis 25:32-33).

Sold!

Here's the root problem in this whole sad tale of a life gone wrong.

Did you know that God said that we'd never be tempted with more than we could bear? Yes, He did! He said that there will never be a situation that leaves us without choice and out of control. God said that we would always have a way to deal with our circumstances without having to compromise and be disobedient.

No temptation has overtaken you except such as is common to man; but God is faithful, who will not allow you to be tempted beyond what you are able, but with the temptation will also make the way of escape, that you may be able to bear it (1 Corinthians 10:13).

There is always a legitimate, godly way of escape from the temptation.

God is Good

I challenge you right now to accept the fact that no temptation comes from God.

Let no one say when he is tempted, "I am tempted by God"; for God cannot be tempted by evil, nor does He Himself tempt anyone (James 1:13).

All good things come from God. When God gives something, it is always good and perfect. Anything flawed or designed to cause you to fall is from satan.

Every good gift and every perfect gift is from above, and comes down from the Father of lights, with whom there is no variation or shadow of turning (James 1:17).

The Scriptures say that there is no variation with God. He stays constant in His nature, and He will not bless you with good and perfect gifts one moment and then try to set you up for failure the next. So, when you face an extreme challenge like the one that Esau found himself in, know this: the author and originator of it is satan, and it is designed to cause you to fall from your destiny. God does not look for ways to see how He can make you fall, but know that He is carefully monitoring your responses to the temptations of satan in your life.

What is this birthright to me? (Genesis 25:32b)

Bang! Right here. This is where he lost it all! He despised his birthright in his heart, and it manifested through his mouth. He put a cheap price on it—he insulted God.

Have you ever been tempted to think that? It seems as though you are going nowhere, and you don't understand the significance of your birthright. You need help now, not later. That's what went through Esau's mind when he made that fatal statement and then acted on it. Well, don't do it. Just keep quiet and wait on God. He'll make a way for you. He has promised to provide escape in any temptation. You see, the temptation is not God's nature, but the escape route is! Hallelujah! He wants to see you win. You are a winner, and you don't ever have to accept second best.

Esau looked the part. He was a man of the land—a hunter. Today we would call him "The Camel Man." The imagination invokes the appearance of a golden-tanned man with his body shaped by the days working the land. Even Esau's body odor was manly and rugged like the land he worked. He was supposed to be the brave and strong one.

On the other hand, Jacob was more the young man in the kitchen. His arms were not tough and hairy, and he was not bronzed by the sun. He was closer to his mother than he was to his father. He was not a man of the land. His countenance was soft and fair. He was not supposed to be the braver of the two.

However, it was Esau who failed the test of courage and buckled under pressure. He was the one who didn't come through. His outer appearance was deceiving. When the rubber met the road, he couldn't hold out. He didn't have what it took to possess his birthright.

Later in his life, it was soft, gentle Jacob who showed an unbelievable amount of courage and heart when he wrestled with the angel at Peniel.

Then Jacob was left alone; and a Man wrestled with him until the breaking of day. Now when He saw that He did not prevail against him, He touched the socket of his hip; and the socket of Jacob's hip was out of joint as He wrestled with him. And He said, "Let Me go, for the day breaks." But he said, "I will not let You go unless You bless me!" So He said to him, "What is your name?" He said, "Jacob." And He said, "Your name shall no longer be called Jacob, but Israel; for you have struggled with God and with men, and have prevailed" (Genesis 32:24-28).

With a dislocated hip he continued to wrestle with the angel of the Lord and refused to let go until he was blessed by Him. His determination to press in was what set him apart.

When I look back on my life, it is evident to me that I was not the one who possessed all the charm and niceties like some of my friends. I was the one least expected to bear fruit in my calling. I was the guy that always said the wrong things at the right time - always put my foot in it. (Whatever it may be that feet go into.) All those guys who gave me no hope have fallen by the wayside, but I'm going on with God. I have watched them fall away over the years as they have despised their holy calling when they encountered their own personal "Esau" experiences. They made bad choices and betrayed their inheritance.

Never Compromise

On the other hand, I have determined in my heart that I will never compromise the gift of God for quick-fix answers. Even at this stage of my life, I still face tough temptations from satan and have to be strong to protect the calling of God on my life. I will constantly be on the lookout for satan, who is always trying to bring me down.

Some Have Fallen Out of the Race

My friend, God is no respecter of persons, and only those who are faithful, even under extreme pressure, will go on to fulfill God's best for them. It is a sad thing to come across believers who have fallen out of the race. I see them everywhere. They've become hardened and offended. They just float around, not growing in their gifts and callings, blaming pastors, Christians, the church, and whatever for their defiance. These dear people aren't verbally denying God. They declare that they are still Christians, but when you look at them, all you see is emptiness. You see people who were once flowing in their anointing but have now somehow become disillusioned. I don't know if this happens in your area, but here where I minister, these folk are found everywhere. Most often, they don't even attend a local church.

Some of them get together and form little groups. They are without a leader and, because they generally have the same issues, they always get into conflict with each other and very soon stumble around again until they join a new group. I feel sorry for these people. They have all the talent in the world, but their character has let them down. They're frustrated and fruitless.

I'm passionate about sonship because I've seen the price of not honoring the inheritance. The price is too high.

Never be fooled by what looks good. So many look the part. They speak well, pray loud,and have all the knowledge but have no courage.

Pressure

Pressure in God's kingdom is like pumping air into a bicycle tube. To find a hole in the tube, you must first fill it with air. The hole in the tube does not manifest until it comes under pressure.

When I was a little boy, I used to fix my own punctures whenever my bicycle had a flat. I would remove the inner tube from the bicycle tire and then blow it up hard. Then I would push the tube under water; when I saw little bubbles rising to the surface from the tube, I knew I had found the puncture.

Only with pressure will the hole in the tube be exposed. While it is flat and there is nothing pushing hard on the walls, the hole will go undetected.

That's how it is with every one of us in God's kingdom. We will come under a lot of pressure to expose weak spots. Sometimes God will stand back and watch the devil bring pressure to bear so that we can see what is really in our hearts. Satan will bring pressure to get us to fail. Satan instigated the circumstances to rob Esau, and he intends for you to fall. God, however, intends for you to stand.

There was pressure on Esau in every way possible, and the deep, hidden values in his heart were made manifest. It's really not difficult to act correctly or to be careful to guard your mouth and heart when things are going well. The true nature of a man is revealed when the going gets tough.

I Want it Now!

Esau said, "*I am about to die,*" meaning that his need was immediate. Now is when he was suffering. Not one day when he gets the inheritance—now. He wanted the need met instantly, and he argued that if his birthright couldn't meet the need immediately, then it was useless anyway. Sure, he said these things under immense strain, but this was the time when he ought to have proved his respect toward his God-given birthright. The statement, "I'm about to die," was not the truth. It may have felt or looked that way, but it certainly was not the truth at all. Likewise, even when it seems that you're at the limit of your spiritual, emotional, and physical endurance, don't let the devil lie to you. It is not the end. God has a way out.

Esau gave up his birthright—just like that! He didn't think twice. He probably thought it was not such a big deal. He would just sort it out later. How deceived can a person be? He sold off his birthright to meet a temporary need. He played now to pay later.

Jacob gave Esau the stew; Esau ate and went on his way.

Something had taken place in the flesh that sent shock-waves into the spirit realm.

Esau was the appointed one. He was the man to carry the mantle. I believe that we should have been saying, "The God of Abraham, Isaac, and Esau," but now we're saying, "The God of Abraham, Isaac, and Jacob." Esau gave it all up without flinching. This has got to rate as one of the ultimate accounts of "bad business" in the Bible.

Flesh to Spirit

The moment that Esau rejected the gift of God for his life in the flesh, his rejection immediately manifested in the spirit. It is as though a line was drawn in the spirit realm, and Esau was never allowed to cross back over again. There was no way that Esau could reverse his action.

You need to realize that every action in the flesh causes a simultaneous response in the spirit. The deal was done and that was that. It was as set as it could be.

We often do things in the flesh, then change our minds and go on as if nothing happened. We assume that just because we no longer feel the same way as we did or we no longer agree with what we did, that all will revert back to the way it was before. This is not true. When we do things in the flesh, there is a corresponding action in the spirit. The action in the spirit is not undone merely because we choose to forget our improprieties or push them aside and forge ahead as if it never happened. People say, "Let sleeping dogs lie," but you must be aware of the sleeping dog because one day the sleeping dog will wake up and bite. You can't make the dog sleep forever.

I have a favorite word—"absolute." It means just that. It cannot be changed. Once Esau made his move, there was nothing that he could do to reverse it. He gave his birthright away. He later forgot about his agreement with Jacob, but that didn't change anything because the issue was settled in the spirit. Remember when Jesus cursed the fig tree? It was settled in the spirit even though it still looked very much alive in the natural. It was only the next day that it actually *looked* dead.

Thus, Esau despised his birthright.

It's Going to Get Tough

I hope you're getting the picture. Bear with me as I attempt to broaden your thinking.

You're going to face some really tough situations in the house. You're going to get fatigued until you think you can't bear it any more. You're going to think that you're emotionally incapable of going further. Your resolve is going to be tested to the extreme. You're going to be weary. You're going to feel like Esau felt.

It's easy to live positively and be all excited about your calling in God when it's going well around you. However, you need to decide now that no matter how tough it gets, you'll not sell out to meet a temporary need!

Weariness will come from many sources. As you flow in the house, the responsibility of it all will tire you. You will become drained as you work in the kingdom. I'm talking about wood-bearing here - being a wood-bearer like Isaac was. There are things that you'll be required to do as a son that will seem beneath you, so beneath your "calling" and "anointing" that it will become just a burdensome chore to you. You'll be tempted to opt out for an easier life or a better opportunity elsewhere.

My worship leader is a true son to me. Once I overheard a conversation that he had on the phone. A call came through to our office from England. A ministry made a direct offer to him to relocate and take up the post as worship leader there. This would be considered a golden opportunity that most people would have seen as an "open door." This young man had been with me from the beginning, when we first planted the church. He knew that he was called as a son in my house and would be with me until my mantle was fully upon him.

I'll never forget his response. He said, "I'm called to be here. I can't even consider it." My heart filled with love and admiration. My trust in him was once again cemented, and I knew that my son is here to stay. Of course, this also magnifies my responsibility to treat him right before God.

Tristan often does the donkey work in our church. I mean he gets into everything that he possibly can. He even collects my children from school on occasion! He cleans, he fixes, he prepares, and he does all sorts of things around the house. And yet, he still leads the entire music ministry. A true son is not afraid to be a wood-bearer in the house.

So Abraham took the wood of the burnt offering and laid it on Isaac his son (Genesis 22:6a).

I know what Tristan must go through sometimes. I was there. I know how it feels when satan throws it up in your face and tells you, "You'll never reach your true potential here. This pastor is just using you. There is so much out there for you where you'll be appreciated and respected a lot more. You don't have to become so tired all the time with this donkey work. It's beneath you. Who do they think you are anyway? They don't respect you."

Your fleshly desires will sometimes speak loudly, but you must make right choices and be a son. God will not allow you to be tempted with more than you can bear. It's great to know that we're actually in a controlled environment and there's a limit to what the devil can do. There is no limit to your ability to stand in Christ. Your ability to stand is greater than satan's ability to tempt. Everything's stacked in your favor. Don't buckle; it's not worth it. The devil wants to bring separation between you and your father in the Lord.

Still Tougher

There will also be times in which you will experience failure. You will try your best and still do it wrong. You'll misunderstand and misinterpret what's expected of you and completely miss the boat. You'll be embarrassed and feel foolish because of your mistakes. You'll look at all this and wonder if it's even worth going on.

You'll feel misused and unappreciated as a son in the house. Often you'll not get any credit for your hard work. Others will be thanked and made a fuss of because of their contribution while your work goes unnoticed. Behind the scenes, you'll be working diligently to further the vision, and others will get the credit. Sometimes you'll be eagerly waiting for the affirmation you so desperately seek for a completed task, but it won't come.

Other times you'll feel so cramped that you'll be bursting to escape and exercise your gifts and talents in the kingdom beyond the confining walls of the local church, and your leadership will say, "Wait, you're not ready."

Still other times you'll be weary as you face discipline in the body. Discipline is never easy nor fun. It's always painful and puts pressure on your flesh.

These things will cause emotional clouds that will rain on your parade and bring a despondency that will attempt to darken your sight so that you lose your vision.

Don't be Hasty

I'm one of those people who has received a big wake-up call about the importance of a good diet. By that I mean, eat the right stuff! We often treat our bodies like our motor vehicles. As long as they are working, it must be OK. Then one day something breaks, and we are shocked to find that it's been wearing out for a long time. If we only took the time to do some maintenance, we could have prevented much future pain. You see, when something breaks that has been wearing out for a long time, it usually affects many other parts also. The problem is complicated and multiplied and takes a lot more fixing than if we had taken the time to do maintenance in the first place.

Because I'm carefully watching my diet, I have made some rules for myself that are not negotiable. One of those rules is this - never eat just anything to satisfy a strong hunger. Why is this? I've taken this stand because I have found that if I'm really hungry and my stomach is screaming at me and I respond to that, I will grab the first thing that I can find to meet the need, and it is typically junk food! So now I pause, ignore my flesh, and wait until I can make a rational decision about what food is available to satisfy the hunger pangs. If I instantly respond to the need, I'm going to find all junk food attractive.

That's what so many fast food outlets trade on. You've heard the saying, "Sell the sizzle, not the steak!" You see, "the sizzle" appeals to the flesh.

I have also made a non-negotiable commitment to maintain myself in the areas of fear, unbelief, and bitterness. I watch myself. I do not entertain wrong emotions. These are more deadly than junk food. I forgive instantly, do not allow fear any entrance, and do not tolerate bitterness in any form.

Esau's response under pressure, while being tempted, broke all the rules. He acted too quickly, so he acted irrationally. Controlled by his needs, he fell into the devil's trap.

He feared. He was afraid and could not trust God. Fear is the opposite of faith. Anytime we fear and act outside of faith we are saying, "God, I don't think that you're able to act for me in this situation. I will make my own plans."

Fight the Good Fight

I have a very special young man who is a son in my house. His name is William. He came from a martial arts background, and he was very skilled in many different martial art disciplines. When he came to us there was a lot of work to be done in his life to set him free. Because of the particular type of ministry that we do, we were able to bring this young man to total freedom. William has now completely renounced martial arts and is a shining example of a good son in the house.

He approached me recently with a very good idea. Based on the need for ministry to the community, William suggested that he offer a self-defense class for ladies and run it under the covering of our church. The course would be presented in purity from a Christian perspective and therefore be an instrument for outreach and contact with the community. I thought it over and gave him the go-ahead. My wife, Lynne, attended the classes and found them exciting.

William started the course with a question that has remained with me ever since Lynne told me about it. He asked, "Is your life worth fighting for?"

The reason that this question made an impact on me was that the Holy Spirit immediately witnessed in my heart with a corresponding question, "Is your *destiny* worth fighting for?"

In his class, William teaches that until you have established in your mind that your life is worth fighting for, all the training and teaching in the world will be worthless.

You see, your destiny and calling in God are going to require a fight. *You* are going to have to do the fighting. The Bible calls this kind of fighting the "good fight of faith." All the seminars, Christian television, gifting, talents, anointing, and even prophecies will not get you through until you are absolute about your determination to fight for your destiny.

Esau had the birthright, but he wasn't prepared to fight for it, so he lost it!

Fight the good fight of faith, lay hold on eternal life, to which you were also called and have confessed the good confession in the presence of many witnesses. I urge you in the sight of God who gives life to all things, and before Christ Jesus who witnessed the good confession before Pontius Pilate, that you keep this commandment without spot, blameless until our Lord Jesus Christ's appearing (1 Timothy 6:12-14).

Notice that Paul was telling his son, Timothy, to fight just as I'm exhorting you to fight. I'm communicating this message to you by the Holy Spirit, and I pray that He makes it revelation to your heart.

In verse 14, Paul further said that he wanted Timothy to keep this command until the Lord's appearing. This tells us that this good fight is a process and is something that we will face throughout life on earth.

During the course that William teaches, he is very careful to present it from a perspective that is devoid of hate, unnecessary violence, and eastern religious factors associated with martial arts. He has taken pains to always teach from acceptable Christian ethics.

Fight Righteously

There is another way to teach self-defense. The goal to survive may be the same, but the method of attaining that goal can be out of line. The method can be filled with hate and violence. It can be with a heart full of bitterness and be driven by evil spirits that display the nature of satan. Is it possible to teach people to act in self-defense in such a way that it displays the nature of God? Sure, it's possible. William does it.

In the same way, I can act in self-defense and fight for my destiny in a way that glorifies God, and He will back me all the way. I can also fall into the trap of trying to fight for my destiny in a way that manifests satan's nature and lose the fight because I'll be on my own!

The Wrong Spirit

I have been witness to the way many sons have had their birthrights stolen from them as the devil has brought temptation their way and they've answered in the wrong spirit. Some rebel against their spiritual leadership and give into bitterness and anger. Some leave their birthright in rebellion because of all the rubbish that satan has laid on them. Others cause division through gossip or manifest satan's nature by causing some to stumble.

I've seen sons in the house rise against their fathers in an effort to sway others to their camp. These manifestations can never be blessed by God because they are driven by fear, bitterness, and unbelief, and they manifest the nature of satan. There are no circumstances that allow for God to bless sin. **A son's goal or final vision may be right, but the action taken to achieve that goal or vision does not automatically qualify for God's blessing and support**. If you try to accomplish a godly goal while bearing fruits of darkness, you're sadly mistaken.

Sometimes Fathers Fail

As a father, I make mistakes. There are times that I misread situations and make the wrong calls. My sons in the house may disagree with me, but they follow my lead anyway. Their positions may even be compromised, but I know and they know that God's hand is able to move despite my human frailty. On the other hand, most of my judgment calls will be correct, even if my sons disagree with them. I understand, however, that to them a perception is truth, even if it is, in fact, wrong. It still remains truth to them from their point of view. This is where trust comes into its own - trust in God to complete in them the job He has started.

My sons will achieve their destiny because they have chosen to fight the good fight of faith and pursue it God's way! You see, their trust is not in me. I am not the source of their purpose. God is. They must obey His principles despite my failings. When it gets tough on their flesh and they don't always understand what's happening, they must fight the desire to fall into the devil's trap. They must never be seduced by anger, independence, rebellion, or bitterness.

How are you known?

Let me ask you a question. Have you ever wondered why Esau was called Edom?

Therefore his name was called Edom (Genesis 25:30).

Why was it even relevant to add this to the scripture?

And Esau said to Jacob, "Please feed me with that same red stew, for I am weary." Therefore his name was called Edom (verse 30).

Esau substituted the stew for his birthright, his destiny. It was a red stew. From that time he was known as Edom. The word Edom means 'red.'

People are known by whatever overcomes them. Another way of saying the same thing is, people are known by the things to which they submit. Esau submitted to the red stew. What are we submitting to? How are we known? How are you known?

I am aware of some people who are known as bitter. That is because they have been overcome by and have given themselves over to bitterness. Therefore, they manifest this ugly aspect of satan's nature.

Some individuals are known as rebellious. This is because they have been overcome by and have given themselves over to a rebellious spirit and therefore manifest satan's rebellious nature.

Likewise, some are known as judgmental because they have been overcome by and have given themselves over to a judgmental spirit and therefore manifest this fruit of darkness.

On the other hand, others are known as loving and kind. This is because they have given themselves to being loving and kind and therefore manifest God's nature.

So, the question you should be asking right now is, "How am I known?"

Don't depend on what you hear. Your friends and associates won't be honest with you unless you insist. Ask someone you can trust to give you an honest answer—someone such as your spiritual father. You may be surprised to hear the truth. Be careful what you submit yourself to; it will determine how you are known.

Let me encourage you. As a son in the house, stay faithful. Be righteous and honorable in your dealings with your spiritual father and the rest of the house. Don't give yourself over to any pot of stew when you're tempted. Don't give up on submission, accountability, faithfulness, and respect. Rather, be ready to experience a father's counsel, discipline, teamwork, and laying of the foundation in your life. Trust God. Don't allow fear or unbelief a chance to gain a foothold. God is in control. Honor the local church and the relationships God has established in your life. This is God's way of preparing you. Don't run out on your birthright when you're tempted to take the low road for an easier deal. That deal is never genuine.

The Father's blessing

A while ago, Clyde, a young man in our church, turned 21 years of age. This called for a celebration. His parents, Tim and Sharron, organized a large gathering of friends and acquaintances.

During the festivities, Tim called Clyde to stand next to him while everyone gathered to hear what he had to say. Tim worked through some typed notes as he spoke prophetically over Clyde's life. Tim declared God's blessings and prosperity over Clyde. He spoke of Clyde's destiny and seemed to be moved by the Spirit as he blessed his son. He prophesied the Word of the Lord over his son, and Clyde was drinking it in.

I was overwhelmed by what I was witnessing. It was powerful. The father was giving his son a blessing as the son was released into manhood. It was a momentous occurrence.

As I watched, I also felt a tinge of sadness. My earthly father had not given me that kind of blessing. I had just sort of drifted from home with no great fanfare. I was left to fend for myself in life without my father giving me a specific blessing the way Clyde was given his. In fact, this kind of thing is very rare in our western culture.

My disappointment didn't last as God gently reminded me that, although I hadn't received a blessing from my biological father, I had received a blessing from my spiritual father when my wife and I were sent out from the local church to plant the church we now pastor. My pastor, his wife, and the eldership of the body laid hands on us, prophesied, and released us. They sent us out as an extension of that house, empowered and equipped with the father's blessing.

I was so intrigued by what had taken place with Clyde that I did some further research on the concept of the father's blessing. What I discovered excited me as I realized with relief that my wife and I had in fact received a great father's blessing from our spiritual father. I was very glad because I want things to be done correctly. The primary goal of the believer should be obedience to God. Part of this obedience is receiving the blessing of the spiritual father before embarking on one's own ministry.

Of Great Value

In Old Testament times, the father's blessing was highly esteemed. It was a momentous event reserved for a special occasion. This blessing gave children a sense of value and security for the future that they wouldn't have without it. When Esau sought the blessing that he had despised and couldn't get it, he became distraught.

And Esau said to his father, "Have you only one blessing, my father? Bless me—me also, O my father!" And Esau lifted up his voice and wept (Genesis 27:38).

We Just Had To Have It!

I never quite knew why, but when we were ready to be sent from my father's house to start our own life as spiritual adults, we just knew that the events of the laying on of hands on us and the sending us out with a word of blessing were so important. It was a defining moment. I couldn't imagine leaving that house without our pastor releasing us with his blessing.

A Release of Power and Authority

Of course, I now understand why our convictions cried out for the blessing. It's God's way. The Spirit would not let us go out into the world without the blessing from the man of God who had fathered us all those years. I am so grateful to Pastor Jimmy for sending us out from his house with his spoken blessing. At that time, neither of us had any idea of the great release of power and authority that took place. That blessing still carries us to this day and will continue to do so until we have completed our journey on earth. That blessing has established a road for us in the spirit. It has set us on course for success and prosperity. Praise God for the father's blessing that rests on our lives.

Falling Short

On the other hand, I have observed those who've left a house in anger and have forsaken their spiritual father's blessing. Since doing so, they have thus far failed to walk in their true calling. They seem to fall short of their vision. They have many natural talents and abilities, but, no matter what they do, they fail to reach the mark. It's uncanny how consistent this pattern is.

There are men and women who are far more gifted and talented than I am who have left the house in their own strength, ignoring the voice of their spiritual father. In time past I walked in the shadow of these people; now I look on them with pity as it is plain for all to see how they've failed in their calling.

The Father's Blessing Makes a Way

Just as I consistently see people who have fallen short of their calling as a result of a lack of blessing on their lives, I have also seen success in the lives of those who have gone out from a house with their spiritual father's blessing. It is as though they're one step ahead all the time; their walk is favored. I see God himself honoring their father's word over them. These folk walk in unusual wisdom and authority. They don't have to strive and battle. They fall into their appropriate, appointed place wherever they go as the father's blessing makes way for them.

I see the father's blessing as a great spiritual ice-breaker. Have you ever been watching TV or a movie and seen footage of those powerful ships that plough through the ice? They can smash a path through thick ice to allow other ships behind them to follow in the newly created space. They make a way for the others where there was previously no way. This is how the father's blessing works. That spoken word will never be lifted. It will forever remain in place. My father's blessing on my life is my own spiritual path-maker. That word always goes ahead of me. The Bible teaches me that God watches over His word to perform it and that it will not return to Him void.

So shall My word be that goes forth from My mouth; It shall not return to Me void, But it shall accomplish what I please, And it shall prosper in the thing for which I sent it (Isaiah 55:11).

God Ratifies the Father's Blessing

When a father speaks a blessing over his son, God honors that word and will act to perform it. You see, God has entrusted this duty and authority to the father. Many people have made a huge mistake by thinking that they can leave their fathers out of the picture and go straight to God. Unfortunately, it doesn't work that way. We can't think that we can honor God while rejecting the structures that were placed in our lives by God himself! The Bible teaches us that we are accountable. I have heard so many rebellious people say, "I don't serve man; I serve God." They say this because they want to communicate that people don't count in their lives. They think that they have some sort of hot-line to God and that spiritual leadership is of no consequence. They want to convince themselves and others that their "hearing from the Lord" is greater than the word of spiritual leadership. These people are living in a fantasy world of make-believe and are on the road to failure. It is delusional for people to imagine that God will place His blessing on them if they've ignored His values.

I have another saying, and sons will do well to hear it, "I don't serve man, but I serve God through my service to man."

Don't just take my word for it--the Bible teaches us that we are accountable to people for our actions.

Obey those who rule over you, and be submissive, for they watch out for your souls, as those who must give account. Let them do so with joy and not with grief, for that would be unprofitable for you (Hebrews 13:17).

I have recognized the importance of the blessing that I'm able to give as a father. I do not give it lightly.

Some Despise the Father's Blessing

My heart has been broken when I've watched sons despise my blessing and turn their backs on God's gift to them. I do not have a high and mighty attitude about myself, but I'm not afraid to call a spade a spade either. The truth is, as a pastor, I am a gift to those whom I father. When sons despise this gift, they're getting on the wrong side of God himself. When they think that they can go down the road to the next pastor and get his blessing, they're badly mistaken. Let me say this emphatically, "No one will have the passion for the well-being of my sons that I have!" The same applies to the pastor down the road. No one will have a passion for the well-being and success of his sons the way he does. When rebellious sons arrive at my door because they've rebelled against their fathers, they will not receive my blessing.

It is a sad thing to see rebellious sons roaming around fatherless. You see, a stranger cannot give a father's blessing. That ministry can only flow through the father. A counterfeit will never carry the weight and power of the genuine.

Paul gave his spiritual son, Timothy, a father's blessing.

Therefore I remind you to stir up the gift of God which is in you through the laying on of my hands (2 Timothy 1:6).

There are some very clear factors unique to the father's blessing.

- A touch from father to son - laying on of hands

- A spoken word from the heart of the father—affirmation through prophecy

- Recognition and declaration of the son's capabilities—releasing of gifts

- Giving the mantle of authority—releasing the son into a special calling

- God himself standing by the blessing—God is witness and empowers the blessing.

Covet the Father's Blessing

I believe that the father's blessing is still vital today. As a son in the house, you must covet that blessing. Make it your business to position yourself to receive it. It is irrelevant how much pride you have to swallow or how much patience it takes. Don't even consider the idea of going on into your own calling in life without it. Ask your father for it. Don't relent; desire that blessing with all your heart. You need that blessing to make a way for you in life in your service to God.

Many times Lynne and I are asked where we obtained all the wisdom, faith, understanding, and courage. I know where it came from. It came from the powerful dynamic of our taking our place in the house as sons and being sent out with the father's blessing. There's no doubt about it!

Too Late

And Esau lifted up his voice and wept. (Genesis 27:38b).

When Esau finally woke up to what he had done, no amount of pleading and anguish of soul could bring back what he had despised through giving in to the flesh.

Lest there be any fornicator or profane person like Esau, who for one morsel of food sold his birthright (Hebrews 12:16).

Notice that the Bible calls Esau a fornicator.

"Any fornicator" This was because he had fornicated spiritually by selling his birthright. The Hebrew word for "fornicator" speaks of male prostitution. He sold something precious and of great value. This is prostitution. He was also called profane.

"Profane person" The Hebrew word for "profane" implies a person who crossed the threshold. When he sold his birthright, he crossed a threshold, and he could never go back over it again.

What would a morsel of bread satisfy in your life? Anger? Offence? Ambition? Rebellion? It's not worth it.

For you know that afterward, when he wanted to inherit the blessing, he was rejected, for he found no place for repentance, though he sought it diligently with tears (Hebrews 12:17).

He found no place for repentance. In other words, no way of going back! His inheritance was gone forever.

Now, some people are going to jump all over me for saying these things. People are going to say I'm being legalistic and that I don't understand grace. Well, Hebrews 12:16-17 is New Testament. These things that I'm sharing with you are prophetic revelation. These are truths and values in the kingdom that we ought to be hearing a lot more about from the pulpit. Of course, these issues are often uncomfortable to hear, but that doesn't justify leaving them out. The church must be bold enough to embrace and declare godly values. If she did so, the church would not get herself into so much trouble!

A Shadow

We understand that the Old Testament is a shadow of the New Testament. Well, you can't have a shadow of something that is not there!

You know that someone is coming around the corner when you see their shadow approaching. The shadow is caused by the real thing. Without the presence of the body, the shadow won't exist. The shadow is evidence of the real body approaching. Similarly, if Israel was a shadow of the church today, then I can accept that a father's blessing in the Jewish culture was a shadow of a father's blessing in the church now. The same truth applies to all the concepts that I'm sharing with you.

Building on Wrong Foundations

I recently spoke to a pastor friend of mine. We discussed a young pastor in his church who decided to leave to plant a church down the road. The thing is, that young pastor was not yet ready and therefore had not been released by my friend. He left without the father's blessing. He also caused division and took some of the father's church members with him. The rebellious young man approached another leader in the area, and this other leader promptly agreed to be his "covering." This enabled the young pastor to announce that his ministry was legitimate.

Of course, it was a matter of time before that young man's heart was pricked. He knew that what he did was wrong and that he was working in his own strength. There was a vital component missing in his life, and he had to find it. I know what was missing—the father's blessing!

He soon found himself in my friend's office. The young man said, "I feel that I want to make things right with you, let bygones be bygones, and move on. Let's be brothers in the Lord and work together." My friend replied, "What you're asking cannot be done because if I let bygones be bygones the way that you're expecting and forget what you did, it will legitimize your actions. You're asking me to give my blessing to bring a sense of rightness to the wrong that you've done. I can't do that. No matter how much I love you, I can't simply let your sin disappear. Unless you repent, it will always be there. I can't make it vanish. You're on your own, without my blessing."

Rebellion = Witchcraft

The rebellious man left, angry and disappointed. That young, self-appointed pastor will never truly have peace in his life. The question is, will God Almighty honor him even although he has built his entire ministry on the foundation of rebellion? No, God will not do that. For

God to do that, He would have to sanction rebellion, and rebellion is as the sin of witchcraft. Did that sink in?

Rebellion is equal to witchcraft in God's eyes. A lot of people have this false notion that they can go anywhere to receive the father's blessing. In other words, if their father won't do what they want, then they'll go elsewhere to get it. Wrong move. Bad idea. Won't work. Nothing can take the place of the true father's blessing. The Lord will not honor a stranger's word over a son when he has rejected his father's word.

I'll say it again using different words this time. People can't expect to have some kind of a direct link to God and by-pass His ordained structures. We as Christians cannot invent our own "righteous" rules, disobey God's values, and then still have the audacity to say we're doing it in *His Name*. It's true; fathers aren't perfect. In fact, many fathers are far from perfect. Many fathers are not good fathers, but that's God's problem. Nowhere in the Bible is sin justified because of another's failure. A man's rebellion cannot be made right because his father has not lived up to his personal expectations.

Some organizations advertise, "Come join us, and we'll give you ministry credentials." So now, many rebellious sons who have despised their father's blessing go to these people and get the credentials as ministers that they so desperately crave. All the credentials and titles in the world are but vanity without the father's blessing.

Sons, hear me today. Value your birthright!

Chapter 5

Wasted Inheritance

As I read this famous parable told by Jesus, I clearly saw a spiritual picture that was given by the Holy Spirit to reveal a truth about sonship. Let Him minister to you as you read this chapter.

Then He said: "A certain man had two sons. And the younger of them said to his father, 'Father, give me the portion of goods that falls to me.' So he divided to them his livelihood. And not many days after, the younger son gathered all together, journeyed to a far country, and there wasted his possessions with prodigal living. But when he had spent all, there arose a severe famine in that land, and he began to be in want.

Then he went and joined himself to a citizen of that country, and he sent him into his fields to feed swine. And he would gladly have filled his stomach with the pods that the swine ate, and no one gave him anything. But when he came to himself, he said, 'How many of my father's hired servants have bread enough and to spare, and I perish with hunger! I will arise and go to my father, and will say to him, "Father, I have sinned against heaven and before you, and I am no longer worthy to be called your son. Make me like one of your hired servants.'"' And he arose and came to his father. But when he was still a great way off, his father saw him and had compassion, and ran and fell on his neck and kissed him. And the son said to him, 'Father, I have sinned against heaven and in your sight, and am no longer worthy to be called your son.'

But the father said to his servants, 'Bring out the best robe and put it on him, and put a ring on his hand and sandals on his feet.

And bring the fatted calf here and kill it, and let us eat and be merry; for this my son was dead and is alive again; he was lost and is found.' And they began to be merry. Now his older son was in the field. And as he came and drew near to the house, he heard music and dancing. So he called one of the servants and asked what these things meant. And he said to him, 'Your brother has come, and because he has received him safe and sound, your father has killed the fatted calf.' But he was angry and would not go in.

Therefore his father came out and pleaded with him. So he answered and said to his father, 'Lo, these many years I have been serving you; I never transgressed your commandment at any time; and yet you never gave me a young goat, that I might make merry with my friends. But as soon as this son of yours came, who has devoured your livelihood with harlots, you killed the fatted calf for him.' And he said to him, 'Son, you are always with me, and all that I have is yours. It was right that we should make merry and be glad, for your brother was dead and is alive again, and was lost and is found' (Luke 15:11-32).

This is a tragic story of wasted inheritance. I have seen this scenario played out before my eyes many times. In fact, once you've been around a while in the Christian faith and have spent some time in the local church, I have no doubt that you'll also recognize this scene. I'm sure that you'll be able to put the names of real people together with actual events and dates in this picture. The reason Jesus didn't use names and places in His parables is that He wanted to enable us to see how our own lives fit into these stories. We are able to insert our own names so that we can learn and grow and embrace the truth.

You and I could be any one of a number of people in this story. We could be the younger son, the older son, or the father. You might even see yourself as the citizen of the foreign country.

Different Vessels

Observe the following:

But in a great house there are not only vessels of gold and silver, but also of wood and clay, some for honor and some for dishonor. Therefore if anyone cleanses himself from the latter, he will be a vessel for honor, sanctified and useful for the Master, prepared for every good work (2 Timothy 2:20-21).

And that they may come to their senses and escape the snare of the devil, having been taken captive by him to do his will (2 Timothy 2:26).

The father in Luke 15 had two sons. They represented two distinct approaches to sonship. Please note the following:

- They represented two opposite principles;

- They had two conflicting attitudes and were two different vessels;

- They were living in the same house;

- They had the same father;

- They had the same choices to make;

- They faced the same temptations;

- They shared the same inheritance.

I have found sons representing both groups in every local church in which I've had the honor of bringing this teaching. No doubt you will experience the same in your church, whether you're the pastor or a son.

*But in a **great house** there are not only vessels of **gold and silver, but also of wood and clay**, some for honor and some for dishonor* (2 Timothy 2:20). (Emphasis added)

To the fathers I say, "Don't go beating yourself up because you've lost sons or they have betrayed you." The above verse says that even in a *great* house there are not only vessels unto honor, but there are also vessels unto dishonor.

Be careful to observe that the presence of vessels unto dishonor does not affect the greatness of the house! Yes, even the greatest houses will have vessels unto dishonor. I've come to accept that God will purposefully send sons with the wrong heart to me so that they may have the opportunity for repentance. God will send them to me so that their values may be challenged. Whether or not they respond remains their choice. I give my best and lay down my life for them, but the decision to change remains theirs. I cannot and will not suffer under a yoke of false guilt if they do not respond to the dealings of God.

God truly loves the vessel to dishonor and will do all that He can to bring about change and repentance.

*Therefore if anyone cleanses himself from the latter, he will be a **vessel for honor**, sanctified and useful for the Master, prepared for every good work* (2 Timothy 2:21) (Emphasis added)

Transition

This verse is talking about transitioning from being a vessel who brings dishonor to becoming a vessel who brings honor. In every house (local church), both of the above vessels are found. The Holy Spirit will constantly work to change vessels who bring dishonor into vessels who bring honor—to transition from being a vessel of wood and clay to becoming a vessel of gold and silver.

The true son in the house, the *yachid*, is the vessel of gold and silver. This can only come about with a **heart** change. If the son's heart is of wood and clay then his life will manifest wood and clay, and he will **be** a vessel of wood and clay. When he repents and changes, his heart will become one of gold and silver, his life will then manifest gold and silver, and he will **be** a vessel of gold and silver. When this happens, it's shouting time in the house. And, boy, do I shout!

To me, the greatest victories have been when I have seen prayer, godly discipline, and love cause vessels of dishonor to change to vessels of honor. I live for those times when I see a heart won over and a right spirit formed. It is then that we can go further and prepare that son for greater things! There is no greater joy in the house for me than to see this transition happen before my very eyes!

*Therefore if anyone **cleanses himself** from the latter…*(2 Timothy 2:21).(Emphasis added)

Sons have to cleanse themselves from the wrong spirit. Don't ask God to clean you. The Bible says for *you* to cleanse *yourself*. The latter refers to the wood and clay that make a person into a vessel of dishonor. Choose today, right now, to be a vessel that brings honor. You can do it. The victory is yours, dear son in the house.

Two Different Sons

Then He said: "A certain man had two sons. And the younger of them said to his father, 'Father, give me the portion of goods that falls to me.' So he divided to them his livelihood" (Luke 15:11-12).

Both sons were heirs of a portion of their father's total wealth. It seems that the two of them were the only heirs to their father's estate.

Now, I'd like you to see the story as the Holy Spirit showed it to me. The father represents the spiritual father in the house. The house represents the local church with the father as the shepherd (pastor). The inheritance is the spiritual inheritance, the spiritual heritage that belongs to every son in the house.

Spiritual Inheritance

Nothing that I am today was accomplished on my own. It also didn't fall out of the sky and hit me on the head. All that God has caused me to become has been founded in the release that came with anointing from my spiritual father. This was and is my inheritance. As I grew in the house as a son, I determined to maximize my time with my spiritual father, Jimmy Crompton. I realized that my spiritual inheritance lay in him. I began to listen to every prophecy he received and then say, "Thank you Lord, that's mine as well!"

I remember when Pastor Jimmy got a word from God that said, "You will touch nations." I said, "Yes, Lord, that's for me, too. He will touch the nations and I'll be running with that anointing as it also flows through me!" When this truth hit me, I didn't bother too much about getting prophecy and encouragement about my future in the ministry. But I took careful note of what God was saying and imparting to my spiritual father because it was all going to become mine anyway. I knew that the blessing that God gave him would be imparted to me. I chose to be a vessel of honor in the house and legitimately possess my inheritance in God. In the same way, I've encouraged my sons to hear what God is saying to me. It's their inheritance. What God pours into my life becomes the spiritual heritage of my sons.

Impatient Son

In the parable, the younger son's heart was not right, and he demanded his inheritance immediately. The timing was premature; he wasn't ready. This was a disaster waiting to happen. I have seen this happen many times when sons have taken the same road as the young man in this parable.

Gift versus Character

It is a great temptation when sons are filled with head knowledge and don't have the necessary spiritual stamina or character to carry them in the ministry. It is so common to see sons in the house become impatient and want to move on. Very often sons do what this son did. They decide that they are ready and mature enough to handle the job, and they demand that the father release them into their calling and give them their spiritual inheritance.

I see many sons who have awesome gifts but who are lacking in character and maturity. They even have a measure of anointing resting on them. God's calling on their lives is evident. Yet, somehow they get restless and grow big in their own eyes. They overestimate who and what they are and push their way into too much responsibility too early and without their father's blessing. Don't confuse gifting with readiness. Gifting grows fast. It is just that, a gift from God. It is free. Gifts mature just because they're there. You can learn to use them and still lack in character.

On the other hand, character must be nurtured. It is not free. There's a price to pay - a very high price to develop great character. You must die! Die to yourself and all that is important to you in order to develop the kind of character that comes from God.

Offences

Still other sons allow themselves to become imprisoned by offences. They are taken captive by the devil and rise up against their fathers in their hearts. They walk out of the house thinking about that covenant relationship in terms of offences in an attempt to legitimize their actions. They say in their hearts, "Well, if I can't do it my way here, I'll just resign and leave." They're in for a surprise. Walking out of the local church for the wrong reasons never brings the desired freedom. It always leads to captivity, as the younger son in Luke 15 soon found out.

Maximize the Inheritance

Sons, don't push and shove to get your inheritance. Be very careful not to force the issue. Wait and allow God to move on your behalf. He will not let you down. I don't know the exact reason why the younger son pushed for his "freedom" when he did. Maybe he had some conflict with his father. I do know this: since the older son was still at home, working faithfully with his father and serving in the house, it wasn't the right time for the younger son to be released into the responsibilities of manhood. The young man just wasn't ready. This is so obvious when you see how ignorantly he dealt with his inheritance, how he wasted and squandered it all on harlotry—a sinful lifestyle.

Your Inheritance is Growing

There is another principle that I would like to bring to your attention. It works like this. Assume a father owns a business and will give half of his business to his son at an appointed time. We will also assume, for the sake of this illustration, that this business grows by 30% per year. Now, the son can see that every year his own inheritance is growing. For each year that goes by before he receives his inheritance, he will inherit more. As the father's net value grows, the inheritance also increases in direct proportion. However, once that inheritance is handed down to the son, that's it—there's no more. Only the remaining portion will continue to grow at the father's hand as he continues to work at his business. The son now becomes wholly responsible to make his own half work and grow. It is his to do with as he chooses.

The same principle applies in the spirit. As a son, I watched how, year after year, the anointing on my spiritual father's life literally multiplied. As I saw this happen, I also saw my spiritual inheritance grow in direct proportion to the growth in my father. The longer I stayed under his roof before I was released into manhood, the better because my portion just grew and grew.

The balance must be right. You must be released at the right time to maximize your inheritance.

And the younger of them said to his father, 'Father, give me the portion of goods that falls to me.' So he divided to them his livelihood. And not many days after, the younger son gathered all together, journeyed to a far country, and there wasted his possessions with prodigal living (Luke 15:12-13).

A short while after the younger son received his portion, he took off. I believe that his newly-found control over his wealth conned him into a false sense of security. He thought that he had it all together and lived it up in a make-believe world of plastic security. I guess his eyes were twinkling and his heart was pounding with the money in his possession. He believed that nothing could go wrong.

Well, as with all the devil's schemes, there is a price to pay. Yup, you can *play* now, but you will *pay* later. It's better to *pay* now and *play* later.

Wasted Anointing?

The word "prodigal" living (*asotos* in the Greek) means "wasteful." He spent his inheritance on wasteful living. Do you know that an anointing can be wasted? Many, many sons have done the same thing as this prodigal son and have wasted their spiritual inheritance.

I have seen how sons have left their fathers prematurely for a variety of reasons with all that they have received, only to realize one day down the road that it's all been wasted. Those sons have little or nothing to show for their spiritual heritage. I do believe that we're all going to be accountable to God for what we've done with our spiritual heritage and how we've valued it.

The Fathers Pay a Price for the Son's Heritage

I've said it so often: spiritual fathers are a great gift from God. It costs these fathers so much to bring sons to maturity. They pay a price that money can't buy. Sure, their reward is in heaven but I want you to know that sons who do what the prodigal son did are going to have to give account for their actions.

The prodigal son despised the inheritance for which his father had worked so faithfully. It couldn't have come easily. I can imagine that the father was already working on that inheritance even before the prodigal son was born! The prodigal wasted it without conscience in a short space of time. How much respect did he show for the years and years of sweat and sacrifice that it cost his father to ensure a future for his son? The prodigal son counted his father's sacrifice as cheap and simply threw it away with wasteful living!

Think about it for a moment.

We so easily do that with our spiritual fathers. If you're about to make a really bad decision, STOP! Count the cost. Value your father in the Lord. Value your inheritance.

Almost Seduced

Let me tell you a story of how a son was almost drawn into the trappings of spiritual harlotry. Spiritual harlotry will cause your inheritance to be sucked dry and wasted.

This young man knew that he had an anointing and gift to preach and expound the Word of God. He was asked to preach from time to time. People would often compliment him and want to know when he was going to preach again. He was confident in his calling and felt ready for the world. He was faithful in the house (local church) but was becoming frustrated. The senior pastor also recognized his gift and told him as much. The problem was that this man's character had not had time to develop, so it was not strong enough to carry his gift. It was clear that his father had not yet considered it time to release him into adulthood. He was not ready to leave and live off of his spiritual heritage. Many in the congregation had told the man to move out. They said that he was wasted in the local church and should go and preach elsewhere whenever the opportunity arose. These influences fueled his frustration and began to give him a big head. A dangerous, underlying arrogance began to creep into his heart.

One day, this young man decided to confide in a friend. The friend was the brother of a famous evangelist who is known worldwide, and the son thought that he would get the right advice from him.

"What must I do?" he asked, "I know that I can preach as well as anyone. People like to hear me preach, and I know that I could make it out there. I feel hemmed in in the local church, and I reckon it's time to go and explore the world."

"Well," the friend replied. "You need to get to America. The Americans will love your particular style of presentation." The friend began to speak of receiving offerings in dollars and spoke mainly of materialistic values, expounding on how this young man could be blessed and really prosper. The friend spoke about all the bright lights and romantic wonders of preaching in the USA. He spoke of becoming a success through correct marketing and the popularity that would follow.

This young man left with sparkling eyes and dreams of becoming a successful preacher in America. It all sounded so exciting! However, something didn't fit. It felt a bit out of place. It was everything that he wanted to hear, but it clashed with his heart of hearts. There was a check. He soon realized that the Holy Spirit was attempting to intervene.

Whoredom

That young man was me. I didn't go to America. I stayed at the local church and grew strong in character to possess my inheritance. Somehow I knew that it would have been a big mistake to go at that time. Today I understand why. Running after the trappings of success, money, and popularity would have been committing spiritual whoredom. The real reason that God has anointed me to do certain things is not so that I can be famous and prosper and have success. It is so that I will use my spiritual heritage to grow His kingdom. My spiritual heritage is there so that I will serve His kingdom with the very gift that He saw fit to place in my care. I am merely a steward and not an owner of the gifts in my life. When my heart's motive is to bless myself with that gift, I'm moving in the same spirit as the prodigal son. Sure, your gift can bring you prosperity. It can and probably will bring you a measure of popularity and favor, but not to assume a position of ownership of that gift. Beware not to squander your spiritual heritage on the pursuit of materialistic and selfish ambition for your own gain.

When I speak of spiritual whoredom, I speak of cavorting with the very things that are the enemies of God. These things include the approval of man, mammon, and popularity.

The prodigal son used his inheritance on harlotry - don't you do the same!

The Famine

But when he had spent all, there arose a severe famine in that land, and he began to be in want (Luke 15:14).

The prodigal son had a wonderful time blowing his inheritance. He must have felt so free and unrestrained. All of his father's control had been shaken off, and the prodigal was determined to live it up. Of course, this exhilaration was a false smokescreen; in reality, he had set himself up for great failure.

There came a famine in the land where he was, and that land was unable to sustain him; he had to look to his own reserves to make it through. Much to his horror, when he looked again, his inheritance had been wasted and he realized that he was in serious trouble.

He began to be in want (verse 14).

His excessive lifestyle began to exceed his resources. Look at the spiritual picture. Sons who run off prematurely with their inheritance, for whatever reason, will enter that realm of false security. Over the years I have observed these men and women who have entertained this spirit and have rebelled. They embark on a road that is littered with casualties. Of course, according to them, their situation is very different from other situations and they have a seemingly justified position. A false confidence sets in. The argument is always similar and the story stale. They spiritualize their excuses until they believe themselves into a trap. They put their trust in a lie and, like the prodigal son, despise their inheritance. They have short memories and forget what it cost their fathers to get them where they are.

Sure enough, when all the fun and laughter settles and the famine descends on the land, they don't have the spiritual depth to sustain them.

Spiritual Reserves

Believe me, every man walks into a spiritual famine in his ministry at some time. By spiritual famine, I mean a famine in the land around him. He must have spiritual reserves within him to sustain him and keep him going while the land around him is in spiritual want. This is the silo of his heart, or rather, his heart is his silo—the place where he stores reserves for the lean times. There is only so much each man can endure until his inner resources run out. If he does not have spiritual depth and strength of character, he will be consumed by the famine. I have found that, as I have been through the famine times, I've walked victoriously and with strength, thanks to the powerful impartation of anointing from my spiritual father. Sometimes even now, years after I was released into manhood, set apart legitimately, and given my spiritual inheritance, I find challenging things come my way. I'm more than equipped to make it through. When those times come, I whisper a "thank you" to the Lord for my spiritual father. I know it cost him to be my father, and I thank him for being prepared to pay the price. I have a rich spiritual heritage, and I'm grateful for that all the time.

Knowledge Alone Won't Get You Through

Don't confuse these spiritual reserves with knowledge. I've met many people with tremendous knowledge. They can preach famous sermons by heart, they know all the good books, they impress everyone with who they know, and they tell of times spent with famous people. But they are so thin in their spiritual depth that if you took all that away from them they'd collapse in a heap. These folk cannot stand in times of spiritual famine. They have nothing in their spiritual reserves. They have learned the "business of the ministry" and have studied the whole system in fine detail. They know exactly what people want and how to say the right things at the right time, but it's all worthless when there is no depth of spiritual reserves. So, knowledge is good, but don't fall for the lie that knowledge alone will get you through.

Sons, don't view all these people as role models and run off to try to be like them. Spend your time in the house where God has placed you to receive your inheritance, and, when God is ready, He will release you with the blessing of your spiritual father. Then you can go out with the blessing and anointing of God with your testimony intact, and you can be an original. Remember, the best that you can be when you try to emulate someone else is No. 2.

You know, I have discovered something interesting. When I left the house I was in to start a ministry, travelling and preaching, the one thing that seemed to open many doors was my testimony of being in one church under one father for 15 years before I was sent out. I was actually surprised that so many pastors commented on this as if it were so unusual. People trusted me and gladly opened their pulpit to me. There is tremendous value in faithfulness. *People trust faithful people.*

The Stranger

Then he went and joined himself to a citizen of that country, and he sent him into his fields to feed swine. And he would gladly have filled his stomach with the pods that the swine ate, and no one gave him anything (Luke 15:15-16).

Here we encounter the saddest part of the story. It's sad for me because I'm looking objectively at the prodigal son's desperate plight, and I clearly see how he's being led by his nose into further deception. This time he's deceived in his expectations. My shepherd's heart cries out for this young man. I can picture him approaching the stranger for help. The stranger wants to help, but not in the way that the prodigal is expecting. The stranger gives him a lowlife job feeding pigs. The young man is shocked. He suddenly discovers that strangers are not going to treat him as his father has. They're all unknown to him, and he's in a strange land. He is someone else's son.

When sons run off to a strange land, they are strangers to those citizens, but they still try to join themselves to those strangers. Look at the situation from the citizen of that land's point of view. If I were that citizen, I would hold to the premise that I am not going to give my son's inheritance to a stranger. The prodigal was a stranger in that land, and they were not going to give him their son's substance; rather, they gave him a job feeding the pigs. He ended up eating the pig's slop.

I have been greatly saddened when I've seen misguided sons head off to strangers in a strange land, wrongly thinking that they're going to get a good deal. Sons never get a good deal from strangers. They get to feed the swine in the field. The tragedy is that it doesn't have to be this way.

Only the Best for my Sons

As a pastor, it is my pleasure and joy to give my sons the very best. I will go to the limits to secure the best for my sons. Those who have taken their place in my house will ensure my faithfulness as a father. There is no way that a stranger will be able to walk in and be given their bread. My heart belongs to my sons. By "my heart," I mean the impartation of anointing that I release. It takes time and commitment to do this, and this time and commitment I gladly give to my sons, not to strangers.

I've seen this situation from both angles. I've had sons leave because they rejected character-forming discipline to go to a strange land and join themselves to a citizen there. They arrive at the other house and lay out their gifts for inspection, expecting to be welcomed and be "more appreciated" than they were at the house from whence they had come.

Others have left their house and come across to my house and have the same attitude. I quickly discern what is happening. Fortunately, I'm a wise father who won't be moved by pedigrees (titles, giftings, etc.). The fact is, it doesn't matter who walks in the door, they do not get the food that belongs to my sons.

Hunger

But when he came to himself, he said, 'How many of my father's hired servants have bread enough and to spare, and I perish with hunger!'

At long last the son sobered up! In a nutshell, he was saying that there was an abundance of food in his father's house and he was a fool to leave like he did. He was starving and realized that the servants in his father's house were better fed than he was.

Depending on your own situation, by now you may realize that you have been spiritually starving since you've walked out on your father. You know that even the men and women with "servant" status in your father's house are being fed with good spiritual nourishment. You may have felt that going to a stranger's house would satisfy the enormous hunger in your heart, but remember that there is more to filling that hunger than receiving the right spiritual information. It's about the father imparting his heart to you.

Pride

Usually, the only thing keeping sons who find themselves in this position from going back to their fathers is old-fashioned pride. Pride can rob a person blind. Don't let pride steal, kill, and destroy all that God has for you.

Sinned Against the Father

I will arise and go to my father, and will say to him, "Father, I have sinned against heaven and before you, and I am no longer worthy to be called your son. Make me like one of your hired servants" (Luke 15:18-19).

There is a tendency among people to bypass the fathers in the house. This is how they do it. They exclude the fathers by saying that their relationship and fellowship are with God only. They believe that they don't "owe any man anything," and they behave as if the fathers are only there to serve and feed them. They live in some weird pseudo-spiritual dimension that they think excludes them from earthly responsibility in the name of being "spiritual" and they call it "being led by the Spirit." Their significance in life is that they believe they have some magical connection to God and that that connection makes their earthly relationships redundant. This perceived super-spirituality makes them haughty and too large in their own sight. This is an attitude that God hates. This is error. To these people, the fathers are merely a commodity to facilitate their purpose. According to them, they're not accountable to the fathers; they're accountable to God only. Every father and son must remember that God certainly works through earthly relationships. They are very important and we are responsible for how we maintain them.

The prodigal came to recognize that, by walking out on his father and wasting his precious inheritance, he had sinned against God. He sinned against God because he scorned God's gift to him. He despised his father and his inheritance that his father worked so tirelessly to provide for him. We need to know that our spiritual heritage is of great value in God's sight. And in fact, how we treat that spiritual heritage does matter very much to God. This is a very serious issue with the Lord.

Even the prodigal son knew this truth. When he finally came to his senses and recognized that he had sinned, he acknowledged his sin before God. He didn't only repent before God (as if his father didn't matter and was an unimportant individual in the biological chain of life), he also repented to his father. Saying "sorry" to God alone was not going to make it right. He knew that God would not have accepted his repentance if he had not also shown remorse for what he had done to his father! In his heart he knew that God Almighty was insulted when the prodigal insulted his father.

People must not be seduced into thinking that they can wound and betray their spiritual fathers and then walk on in life as though it doesn't matter. It does matter. It matters to God. God expects us to make these things right.

And he arose and came to his father. But when he was still a great way off, his father saw him and had compassion, and ran and fell on his neck and kissed him. And the son said to him, 'Father, I have sinned against heaven and in your sight, and am no longer worthy to be called your son' (Luke 15:20-21).

The prodigal son finally decided to return and repent before his father. He must have been shocked at his father's reaction of running to greet him and showering him with love. The son only expected to be treated as a servant. Instead, he was greeted with his father's love and forgiveness.

The Love of a Father

The father's reaction doesn't surprise me in the least. Allow me to share from my heart and to speak from the point of view of a spiritual father of many sons in my house. I wish to communicate something to you that most sons don't comprehend, and that is the capacity for a father to love intensely, to the point that it seems detrimental to his own well-being.

I have personally suffered tremendous emotional pain that only the power of God could heal as I've seen some sons in my house do what the prodigal did. I've been betrayed, abused, and used by many who have only pretended to be faithful sons. The dilemma that I face is that I don't know which road the sons are going to follow when we start out - the high road or the low road. So, I've had to make a choice. I've had to choose to love unconditionally. I've had to come to the place where I walk without fear of being let down. I've had to realize that every individual has the power of choice. It is in their power to make good or bad choices. Some sons are going to make choices that I know are wrong and are going to cause me pain. Some fathers have been so broken by betrayal that they've become afraid of being hurt. Some have even been used to the point that they've become offended and angry. Unfortunately, this anger and bitterness is not selective, and it shows in their dealings with all their sons in their house. I've had to come to terms with these issues in my own life. Once I determined never to walk in bitterness toward those who have betrayed me, the love of God enveloped my heart.

The Pain of Lost Sons

Here, I can identify with the prodigal's father. I've had sons leave me, deserting the house for all the wrong reasons. Some of these experiences have brought me to tears and to my knees as I've wept before God because the pain of the loss has been so traumatic. I've thought to myself, "Well, if they've wanted to hurt me, they've got it right." I've almost cursed the day I gave my heart away to disciple these sons. However, when I let God the Father's heart envelop mine, I came to know what it's like to stand at the gate and wait for those sons to return, longing for them as only a father can.

The anguish I go through for these sons is two-fold. First, the anguish is for them because I fear what will happen to them. I know that if they get their way and continue to walk the walk they've chosen, they will, like the prodigal, lose so much. It breaks my heart to see the ones I love be seduced and drawn away. I know how much I have to give and how much I want to give it to them.

Second, the anguish comes as a result of their separation from me. When sons break relationships with me, it's like a tearing in my soul. It's never easy. Betrayal is one of the hardest and most difficult wounds to bear and heal. It strikes deep in the human heart. When we are betrayed, we struggle with our identity and self-worth.

I pray for my lost sons all the time. I'm like a parent who sees his children out there and longs to have them back.

So, I want you sons to know that your spiritual father loves you. There is something that God puts inside a shepherd that is unshakable. It is a love for his flock. I will die for my people. In fact, I've walked that route already, but that's another story. My appeal to sons is that you must believe in your heart that your spiritual father loves you intensely. If he doesn't always show it, be patient and try to understand that he may have been betrayed very badly and is weary in his soul. He needs your love in return. You may just be the one to restore his heart and encourage him to trust again.

No matter what my sons have done or where they've been, there remains a love in my heart for them that is unbreakable - just like the father of the prodigal.

Rejoice!

And he arose and came to his father. But when he was still a great way off, his father saw him and had compassion, and ran and fell on his neck and kissed him. And the son said to him, 'Father, I have sinned against heaven and in your sight, and am no longer worthy to be called your son.' But the father said to his servants, 'Bring out the best robe and put it on him, and put a ring on his hand and sandals on his feet. And bring the fatted calf here and kill it, and let us eat and be merry; for this my son was dead and is alive again; he was lost and is found.' And they began to be merry (Luke 15:20-24).

When the prodigal finally returned, the father ran to the son, fell on his neck, and kissed him. This is not an unexpected reaction in the light of what I've just shared.

Oh, hallelujah! What great and awesome rejoicing when one of my sons comes home. Of course, the best robe, ring, and sandals must be put on him. All must celebrate and dance with joy because the lost son is back. Bring the fatted calf and let the feast begin in honor of the returned son!

The father said, "*For this my son was dead and is alive again; he was lost and is found.*" The severity of the pain in the father's heart was great, so the joy at the return of his son was proportional. That's why he likened this experience to someone coming back from the dead. It felt just that way! I know the joy in that father's heart at the return of his beloved son.

Now his older son was in the field. And as he came and drew near to the house, he heard music and dancing. So he called one of the servants and asked what these things meant. And he said to him, 'Your brother has come, and because he has received him safe and sound, your father has killed the fatted calf' (Luke 15:25-27).

The place lit up with merrymaking. I've seen sons return to the house where they belong, and the church lights up with gladness. There's happiness in the air that spreads to everyone in the flock. It's a wonderful day.

But he was angry and would not go in. Therefore his father came out and pleaded with him. So he answered and said to his father, 'Lo, these many years I have been serving you; I never transgressed your commandment at any time; and yet you never gave me a young goat, that I might make merry with my friends. But as soon as this son of yours came, who has devoured your livelihood with harlots, you killed the fatted calf for him' (Luke 15: 28-30).

The Faithful Son

Here's a dilemma that many have not understood. I have seen many people come down on the older brother. He's often judged and left out in the cold because his attitude was out of line.

I would like to show you that the older son was, in fact, the faithful one in the story. Sure, his character needed some honing, but he wasn't the one who wasted his spiritual heritage.

I was once in the same position. I also needed some teaching from my spiritual father to clear up the matter for me. I was going through a bad time and was feeling neglected and disgruntled. I was upset because I wasn't getting the attention I felt I deserved. The pastor was spending more time with other leaders in the church, and I felt left out in the cold. I spoke to him and said, "I don't see why I have to just carry on and, as long as the job gets done, I never get to see you or spend time with you. The only input I receive from you is the occasional 'are things OK?' It's your standard expectation that I'm going to report that 'everything's fine' and then that's the end of your input."

He said, "You know, Jerome, when I give you something to do, I know that it's in good hands. You've proved yourself to be capable and trustworthy. Frankly, I didn't realize that you needed my attention because it *looked* like you didn't need it." As we spoke further we both recognized that I had a need, even though it didn't seem like I needed his attention.

From the father's point of view, he didn't have to make a fuss of me. I was already his son. It was as if I had graduated to a level where I no longer needed "babying."

Two things happened.

One, the father saw a need in me that he hadn't seen before.

Two, I saw that my attitude was wrong and the father wasn't rejecting me. What I now saw was his *confidence* in me! I realized that I didn't need to be jealous of those with whom the father spent more time. There was good reason for this and it had absolutely nothing to do with acceptance or rejection of me. I was set free.

The older son in this parable suffered the same emotional upheaval when he saw the younger son getting all the attention. He experienced a wave of jealousy and reacted to it. He thought he was also protecting his father's interests. I think he was really bent out of shape because, in his opinion, he deserved a lot more attention. He was correct when he said that he had been faithful while the younger brother had not. In the flesh, he had reason to be angry. It's easy for us to jump all over the older brother in our sermons and illustrations but until we've actually experienced what he'd been through when his brother left, we'll fail to understand his perspective. Sure, he was wrong to become angry and needed to change his attitude, but let's remember what he had to deal with at that moment.

Sons Working as a Team

Here's something else to consider. The family business was a team effort. The father and both sons were working well together. When there is a team working at something and one of the team breaks rank, the workload always increases for all the remaining team members.

To illustrate, our music team had grown into a phenomenal unit. The spiritual chemistry was awesome, and God was blessing the team greatly.

Everybody was giving their best and flowing at full throttle. Suddenly, a young woman on the team began developing problems. I, together with the worship pastor and others in the team had poured our lives into her, believing in her future ministry and destiny. The gifting and anointing of her music ability was of an unusually high quality. However, her character needed a lot of work. Her husband had let her down, and she began to look to the males around her for comfort. This became a problem. I had to intervene before there was irreversible damage. I loved her as if she were my very own daughter. I placed her under two women in our church for a time of discipline to bring healing to her life. These two ladies attempted to take her through a process called "soul care" (which my wife leads). During this time, she was not be play and sing on the music team until these two ladies gave me the go-ahead that she had become emotionally strong enough. The Holy Spirit told me to keep her from receiving ministry from any male figures at this time. She was not being punished but being placed in a safe position for her own protection.

The Team is Let Down

She immediately rejected this idea and walked out. This action broke my heart, but I was committed to obeying my responsibilities as the pastor, even to the point of my own loss. I was not going to compromise and therefore lost one of the most cherished sons whom God had given me.

The snowball effect was obvious. The workload on the worship pastor immediately multiplied. Now, remember that he's the faithful son, the one who has never even contemplated doing what this young woman had done. He stayed with me through thick and thin and served faithfully in the house. He did not deserve what he got. When this young woman ditched us, the worship team and, more specifically, the worship pastor, had to absorb her workload, thus paying a great price because of her rebellion.

Let's look again at things from the older son's perspective.

The older brother in the parable was angry because, when the younger brother ran out on his father, he also ran out on the brother. The brother and father were left with a heavy workload while the younger man was living it up, wasting his inheritance and rejecting his responsibility. It is understandable that the older brother was annoyed. He felt done in and cheated.

"Why is my father now acting as though the other son is the big hero, when everyone is well aware of how the two of us suffered because of my younger brothers' ungodly actions?" he might have thought.

There may be times when we all feel this same way. For me, in the situation described earlier, I experienced peace in my heart when I understood that my place was cemented by the Holy Spirit.. I was no longer threatened when I wasn't the one getting the attention. I became confident in my role as a son in the house. I clearly understood that, as long as I guarded my heart and kept the right attitude, God would ensure that my destiny would come to pass. I watched sons come and go, but I stayed there, faithful, until I was released to go in a godly and scriptural way.

Inheritance Lost

And he said to him, 'Son, you are always with me, and all that I have is yours. It was right that we should make merry and be glad, for your brother was dead and is alive again, and was lost and is found' (Luke 15:31-32).

Here's the thing. The father said, "*You are always with me, and all that I have is yours.*"

"All that I have is yours" meant just that. You see, the father had divided up the inheritance between the two. The younger son spent his. All the remainder belonged to the older, faithful son.

The following fact is hard to accept but nevertheless is the truth. **There are some decisions in life from which we cannot come back**. We can be forgiven, welcomed back, and have the past put behind us, but we can't replace a wasted inheritance.

The father of these two boys rejoiced and killed the fatted calf when his son came home. He was overjoyed at his return and rightfully so. There's one thing, however, that the father could not do. Despite the fact that he put a robe around him, put the ring on his finger, and put sandals on his feet, the father could not restore his younger son's wasted inheritance. In his father's eyes, he was dead and now was alive; he was lost and was now found. However, the son's inheritance was spent and wasted on harlotry. All the love and passion of the father could not restore it to his son. I repeat, there are some decisions from which people do not come back, and there are sons out there wasting their inheritance. We can only pray that they come home before it's all gone.

Chapter 6

The Fathers' Nakedness

I hope that this chapter will change the way you look at your spiritual father and that it will help you to be at ease with your father's weaknesses. In addition, this chapter is intended to expose the dangers of a wrong attitude toward your father in the Lord.

And Noah began to be a farmer, and he planted a vineyard. Then he drank of the wine and was drunk, and became uncovered in his tent. And Ham, the father of Canaan, saw the nakedness of his father, and told his two brothers outside. But Shem and Japheth took a garment, laid it on both their shoulders, and went backward and covered the nakedness of their father. Their faces were turned away, and they did not see their father's nakedness. So Noah awoke from his wine, and knew what his younger son had done to him. Then he said: "Cursed be Canaan; a servant of servants he shall be to his brethren." And he said: "Blessed be the LORD, the God of Shem, and may Canaan be his servant. May God enlarge Japheth, and may he dwell in the tents of Shem; and may Canaan be his servant" (Genesis 9:20-27).

Laboring in the Vineyard

And Noah began to be a farmer, and he planted a vineyard (Genesis 9:20).

The vineyard that Noah planted was not for him. It was for his family. He planted and then labored in that vineyard so that his family could have sustenance. Yes, he farmed and planted for the benefit of his family.

As a pastor I have come to understand that kind of labor. I do not labor for myself. No sir, I labor, of course, first and foremost, for my God who has called and commanded me. In His Name, I am called to feed His sheep. I am obligated to lay down my life for the sheep, specifically for those over whom God has made me shepherd. To this end, I have labored to provide sustenance for His sheep. This is my reasonable service. Noah became a farmer and planted a vineyard to provide sustenance for his sons. Likewise, I have planted and now labor in a vineyard to provide sustenance for my sons. This vineyard that I work is the ministry to which I'm called. It is the church that I pastor plus all the satellite issues that are attached. This vineyard work is really strenuous and often grueling. I mean, it's tougher than anyone said it would be. It's also often thankless, unappreciated, and misunderstood.

At other times this work is taken for granted. Similarly, Noah likely went into that vineyard day in and day out while his family may have overlooked how much effort it took to maintain it. Only *he* would be familiar with the long, hot days in the sun as he tirelessly worked to provide for his house. It would have been tough out there, struggling with fatigue and battling against the elements to plant and grow that vineyard. It must have taken an untiring and dedicated commitment to farming to see it bear fruit to feed his family. Now I know how fathers think, because I am one. As a family man, I work hard to provide, but I don't expect my children to repay me in any way. It's my reasonable service and my pleasure. All I ask is that they understand when I come home tired that I need the freedom to do what tired people do—rest. I don't expect them to even know what I've done and the effort I've put into the work. As a husband and father, my reward is the satisfaction of knowing that my family is cared for. I do not expect any sort of repayment for this sacrifice. In fact, I try to keep all those details to myself. Sometimes my work causes me great pressure. I understand my role as husband and father and my family's role of wife and children. I, therefore, try to avoid the situations in which these pressures, and any of the burdens of my labor, may transfer onto my family.

My role as a pastor holds similar values. As I've indicated, I gladly labor on that vine that I have planted as a farmer in God's kingdom. I have accepted the fact that the same values that I've just mentioned apply here as well. My congregation will never really have a true perception of the price I pay to maintain and grow this vine, and neither do I expect this of them. It is true that I have many faithful sons who are standing beside me, but the ultimate responsibility of successfully farming the resources that feed the whole body rests on me. It is my choice and privilege to undertake this role as God has required of me.

Taking it for Granted

However, I find that many people of God take it for granted that this vine will be there. They think of its presence as if it's their right to have it. The cost of the availability of this vine that gives sustenance to the body is largely not appreciated by those who live off of it. They have no clue as to what it costs to plant and work the vineyard. The absolute sacrifices made by those functioning in the role of fathers are often ignored. The vine is the lifeline for the church. It feeds the church. Sons should have respect for the sacrifice made, even though they can't quite quantify the price that is paid to provide it for them.

A Gift

The Bible teaches us that the governmental ministry in the church is given as a gift from God.

And He Himself gave some to be apostles, some prophets, some evangelists, and some pastors and teachers, for the equipping of the saints for the work of ministry, for the edifying of the body of Christ (Ephesians 4:11-12).

I believe that a mark of good sons is a healthy and honest respect for the office of the governmental ministry that God has called to father them.

In contrast, the concept that fathers are simply in this to benefit themselves has often crept into the minds of sons. Some sons become suspicious and leave the door wide open to receive offence.

Drunkenness

Then he drank of the wine and was drunk (Genesis 9:21a).

Noah got drunk. He got drunk from wine consumed from the vine that he planted. He then became naked in his tent as a result of his drunken state. So, in a nutshell, to sustain his family and live out his purpose as a husband and father, he planted a vine and drank of the wine from the vine, which led to him being naked in his tent.

God has used this incident to reveal spiritual truth to me about a father's work in his house.

The vine is the work—the church that I pastor. It is the sum of all the factors that make up the ministry I lead. I do not work this work for myself but for those whom I pastor. I am a shepherd, and I understand and accept that my life is not my own. It is a life surrendered and a life that I choose to lay down for the sheep. The vine that I labor in is there to provide for them.

Wine – Bitter and Sweet

Now, this vine produces wine. Like Noah, I and all fathers in God's kingdom consume this wine. The wine is the fruit of the vine. It is what the vine produces and gives. A consequence of planting, growing and maintaining this vine is the consumption of its wine. The result is drunkenness.

This might sound really strange to you—speaking about drunkenness and all. Please understand, I do not in any way support or endorse drunkenness in the flesh. Become as drunk as you desire in the Spirit, as far as I'm concerned, but stay away from the heavy stuff in the flesh. I am referring to "getting drunk from the wine of the vine" as a metaphor.

When God revealed this to me, I became aware of just what this wine is. This wine is bitter and sweet at the same time, and it induces drunkenness.

Bitter Wine

The bitter taste comes in many forms. When people betray me, lie about me, misuse me, break me down, misinterpret me, slander me, blacken my name, falsely accuse me, and use other forms of attack on my person because of the ministry, it has great emotional impact on me. The drunkenness is the emotional pounding that I endure in these circumstances.

Emotional Strain

Most of the time I will be under an emotional load as I put a great deal of effort into helping people when they're in trouble or when they suffer trauma or tragedy. Most people have no idea how much a father takes on in the house. Consider this. You can take any given moment in time in a church and there will be at least one person or family going through some type of trauma or trouble. The shepherd cannot help becoming emotionally involved. Most of these folk act as if they're the only ones in need. When their need is met, their perception is that the shepherd's problems are over. Of course, this is not true. First, there are always a number of families in need at any given time and second, as soon as one need is met, others arise. The wellbeing of the sons lays heavily on me because I am a father, and I love them. I get drunk from the consumption of this bitter wine.

At War

At other times it is the wine of warfare that makes me drunk when I confront great opposition to the gospel and to the ministry. When the gospel is being threatened, I respond by placing myself in the firing line to defend the territory.

Discipline

Sometimes attacks come from within. I embrace my responsibilities as a father and have to exercise discipline in the lives of those in the flock who have stepped out of line. I do not enjoy these times. I would rather avoid these confrontations and hope they go away. I know, however, that the long term damage that will be caused by doing nothing will be too great a price to pay. So, I've learned to be wide awake at all times. As difficult as it is, I have to intervene with discipline when it's necessary. Exercising discipline is extremely emotionally draining and brings more wine and more drunkenness.

Watchfulness

I'm constantly on guard duty—always alert for the enemy's strategy to infiltrate and strike at the sheep in my fold. I'm watching for their safety and wellbeing. When they take hits, I feel it and drink wine from the vine, bitter wine that makes me drunk.

Heartache

The loss of a son, who turns his heart against me in betrayal, results in a particularly deep pain and anguish. This form of drunkenness has been the worst for me to handle. Just because I conceal it well does not mean that the deep wound is not there.

Sweet Victories

The bitter wine that leads to drunkenness would be nearly impossible to bear were it not also for the sweet wine. The sweet-tasting drinks from the vine are the victories that I experience, the simple happy experiences as a father in the house. These experiences are in the majority. In other words, the wine is far sweeter than it is bitter. There are so many more wonderful, faithful sons whom God has given me than those who are disloyal and those that bring offenses. There are so many more that respond to loving, godly discipline than those who reject discipline and rebel.

All the wonderful things that God constantly does in the growing of this vine are also sweet tasting. More often than not, I'm in a place of great excitement and joy from answered prayer as God has once again moved miraculously and wrought a great victory.

The bliss of restored marriages, the overwhelming ecstasy experienced when the heart of a wayward son is restored, the awesome glory of a great battle won in the church finances, the excitement of seeing a broken captive set free by the power of Jesus, and many other positive experiences constitute the sweet wine from the vine that leaves me euphorically drunk.

Consuming the Fruit of the Vine

Every person involved in any sort of ministry will experience this consumption of the fruit of the vine. Every pastor will clearly identify with the realities about which I've just been speaking. These simple examples can give sons a clearer picture of the type of things that make up the wine that is consumed in the growing and maintaining of the vine. Their spiritual fathers get drunk from this wine. I want sons to see that life as a father is not just a glorious ride. I want sons to know that, despite what fathers may portray, maintaining the vine is not just a carefree walk in the park.

Sons, your father in the Lord needs you to be there for him.

Naked

And became uncovered in his tent (Genesis 9:21b).

As a consequence of drinking the wine from the vine, Noah became naked in his tent. Nakedness speaks of exposure and vulnerability. The drunkenness caused Noah to be exposed. He lay in his tent, vulnerable and revealed. He was at the mercy of those prepared to enter his tent and look on.

Drunkenness renders a person ***defenseless***. Noah was lying in his tent and, because of his drunken state, he was not able to act in authority. This was the moment of his total weakness. Yes, he was weak in the flesh, and his capacity to defend his situation had been dramatically reduced by the drunkenness that had enveloped him. He was unable to take control and protect himself against this most embarrassing situation in which he found himself. I think that when he became drunk, Noah recognized his defenselessness and withdrew to his tent.

The Bible describes his state in his tent using the work "uncovered." His clothes had covered him, hiding the person underneath. In contrast, being uncovered speaks of the removal of the things that protected him from exposure.

His tent was his only defense. It was his own personal and private space, and entrance was by ***invitation*** or by ***association***. In other words, those who were in a place of privilege and trust were the ones who had access to his tent and therefore were privy to Noah's nakedness. If Noah was to feel safe anywhere, it would have had to be in his tent - his place of refuge in his time of need.

In the world of the ministry today, the wine from the vine will sometimes induce drunkenness in the fathers. The drunkenness that overtakes the fathers will cause them to become exposed as their metaphorical nakedness is revealed to the sons. The sons in the house are privileged to have access to the father's personal space, and it is here that they will see things that disappoint them. They will see their preconceived religious and idealistic image of what a father should be crumble as the father's humanity is revealed in his drunkenness.

Fathers – Perfect People?

There is a tendency among congregations to expect pastors and others in spiritual leadership to always behave in a precise and perfect way at all times. They don't realize that these men and women, who have taken up the extreme challenge of spiritual leadership and responsibility, are ordinary people with desires, dislikes, and feelings like everyone else.

They experience the same pains and emotions as their sons. People in the ministry did not undergo some magical translation into super-humans the day they entered into the office in which God placed them.

I accept that fathers have a greater accountability. I also accept that fathers are expected to have a far more mature disposition. They are expected to lead by example. This, however, does not mean that they will never be vulnerable and exposed.

Sons, you will see your father do strange and inconsistent things in his drunken and naked state. You will see his excessive joys and excitement at victories. You will see indiscretions and mistakes as he gets drunk in the battle. He will forget things and remember the wrong things. While he's naked he can't really help himself. There will be times when you'll see him hammered by pressure and buckle under the load. At this time he might display some less than perfect behavior. Drunken people do that. During this time he will not behave perfectly.

Drunkenness often occurs when there is an accumulation of disappointments over a period of time. I sometimes feel like a boxer in the ring. When I enter the ring for a new fight I'm fresh and ready to go. There's a bounce in my step, and I'm sharp and thinking clearly with the goal of victory firmly in my sights. As the fight wears on, I take blow after blow. I absorb the first few blows fairly comfortably. After a while, though, I feel dazed. As the blows keep coming, I struggle to stay on my feet. The only thing that keeps me going is the knowledge that I'm assured of victory.

Fathers in the body of Christ go through a similar experience in the ministry. The betrayals, heartaches, etc. take a toll on them. One hit after another comes, and the fathers get so knocked about that they can hardly stand. This results in drunkenness setting in and causing them to become vulnerable and exposed. At this time they look weak, and they may lose their hero status in their sons' eyes.

Now, I'm not speaking here of moral misbehavior. I don't mean that the drunkenness will justify sexual immorality, thievery, lying, greed, and the like. Nakedness refers to the humanity of the fathers, their frailty in the face of battle and victory, and their responses to the emotional situations in which they become involved.

The Wrong Spirit

And Ham, the father of Canaan, saw the nakedness of his father, and told his two brothers outside. But Shem and Japheth took a garment, laid it on both their shoulders, and went backward and covered the nakedness of their father. Their faces were turned away, and they did not see their father's nakedness (Genesis 9:22-23).

When I read what Ham did, I get the idea that he looked intently on his father's nakedness. This may not seem like such a big deal at first glance, but when I relate it to personal experience, I can understand why his behavior was so despicable. There are some things that are difficult to put into a simple doctrinal "right and wrong" and this is one of them. What you need to see here is the spirit in which things are done.

To Justify Offence

When a son becomes offended in his heart, he will begin to look for issues to attack. He'll begin to probe the life and character of his father in order to give credibility to his sinful heart. There is no doubt in my mind that anyone who determines to find fault in me or any other father in the body of Christ will do so. All he has to do is use his place of relationship and privileged insight into the father's life, and he will be successful in his quest. He will find fault. He will not only find fault and weakness, but he may find fault that he feels warrants a genuine scriptural accusation.

Using Privileged Position

"Aha!" I can just hear the son with the hardened heart as he discovers faults and weaknesses in the father. The deception here, though, is that this type of behavior will provoke God to anger because that son has placed himself as judge and executioner of his father in the Lord. Many people think that hauling out a scripture to prove the father's guilt and expose his nakedness constitutes a legal ground in God's sight! How mistaken they are! God will not accept a son's case when his spirit is evil.

On more than one occasion I've had sons with those evil hearts attack me. The thing is that I find myself defenseless because they use their privileged position against me. How do they do that? Well, for a period of time we have a good relationship. They draw close to me as I welcome them in. A relationship of trust develops. I begin to relax in their presence. I begin to "unwind" within their sight. They see me naked.

They look on my nakedness when I am made drunk from the vine. All seems well until one day they suddenly develop an offence. The offence penetrates their hearts and becomes a root of bitterness.

Next they want to defend their evil offence. I feel that what I am about to tell you, at this point, will change your life forever. Whether you heed or ignore the words, you will inevitably reap great fruit, either for great blessing or for great cursing.

These sons go on the attack and begin to degrade me, using my human weaknesses to which they were exposed when I was rendered drunk from the wine of the vine. These attacks come viciously, and the grieved sons immediately begin to report the nakedness to others, attempting to transfer their offence and defend their case by exposing my weakness in the moment of my defenselessness. They glory in their "scriptural" proof of my inadequacies and failures.

The thing is, I'm not denying the scriptural basis of my failure. I'm not even in a position to say I'm perfect and I haven't failed. In fact, I'm at a loss for words or defense because I know that I have been wrong and weak when found naked. When this happens, what can I say? What really wounds fathers is that sons will live in the house for years, and their father's nakedness will never be an issue or reason for offence. This is because, at that time, the relationship is built on the correct principles. Suddenly a son will become offended, and the very things that the father trusted the son with, the son now uses as weapons to attack the father. The evil-hearted son knows full well that his father has absolutely no defense against this sort of attack.

So, let's get back to Ham.

He saw the nakedness of his father, looked on, and then went and announced it to those outside. My question to you is, "Was God more angry with Noah for getting drunk from the vine, or with Ham for abusing his father's nakedness?"

I suggest to you that Noah becoming drunk from the vine and his subsequent nakedness wasn't the issue with God. The bigger issue was Ham's attitude.

Sons, you must be very, very, very careful how you handle what you see when your father's nakedness is exposed to you, as you've been allowed into his inner space in your relationship with him.

Critical Spirit

One should not allow a critical watchdog attitude to set in. Do not take it upon yourself to criticize your spiritual father. Some people are just a pain. All they want to do is find fault, and boy can they dig! They position themselves to observe all the little mistakes so that, as self-styled critics in the house, they can expose them. They will stand and look on the father's nakedness and point the finger. These individuals seem to walk under a permanent yoke of offence. If you know people like this, then you ought to avoid them lest that spirit come on you.

A Godly Attitude

But Shem and Japheth took a garment, laid it on both their shoulders, and went backward and covered the nakedness of their father. Their faces were turned away, and they did not see their father's nakedness (Genesis 9:23).

Shem and Japheth also had access to Noah's place of privacy where he was exposed. In contrast with Ham, we see two different attitudes, two different reactions, two different values, and two different results.

Where do you stand with your father today? What are you doing with his nakedness?

I have come to the place where I've accepted that some sons are going to abuse their position of closeness. I think it's a special thing when sons are my sons in their heart of hearts even when they've seen me naked so many times. I understand that it's not always easy for sons to see their fathers in their weakest, most defenseless state of drunkenness and still remain faithful in their hearts. The thing is, can I say that a son's heart truly belongs to me when he's only seen the controlled side of me? Think about it. How do you want to know your father? As the ultimate "Mr. Perfect" with every hair in place and always shining? As "Mr. Perfect Manners" who's always right and never misses a beat? As "Mr. So-Good" who makes you feel like such a nobody and a failure in his presence? As "Mr. I-Know-Everything" who's always superior to you? Or as "Mr. So-Super-Anointed" who compels you feel as if you should bow when he comes in? I don't think so!

The issue isn't about being exposed to your father's nakedness. It's about what you do with it.

My wife and I have often had young men and women living in our home. I don't mean for a weekend but rather, at times, for a few years. We've considered the fact that, in doing this, we stand completely exposed. We know we're going to do things and act in ways that will not always seem so "spiritual." I remember when one of my spiritual sons, Tristan, who is now a pastor in our church, lived in our home. During that time there was an incredible amount of pressure on us from all sides. We had recently arrived in a strange place and had been thrown in the deep end to pastor and plant the church from scratch. So, needless to say, both my wife and I would at times became very drunk from the vine and became naked. (Now, now, don't you laugh - you know what I'm talking about here!) We went through a tough time in our marriage, and things would often boil over in our drunken state resulting in conflicts and arguments. I don't have to tell you that marital disputes can be very verbal and clamorous.

Sometimes Tristan would be in the proximity of these conflicts and be exposed to our nakedness.

Their faces were turned away, and they did not see their father's nakedness (Genesis 9:23b).

Tristan would simply make himself scarce and disappear. He was, and is, a good son. We successfully made it through that difficult time of drunkenness and nakedness in our lives. How damaging it could have been if Tristan chose to look on and then broadcast the news of the pastor's nakedness that he had observed.

Your Decision

You must decide now what you're going to do. There will eventually come a time when you will come across your father, drunk and naked. How will you respond? Will you stand, look on, sneer, and despise his weak, defenseless disposition? Will you consider his nakedness as ammunition to use for your own gain? Will you try and use his nakedness to justify your own rebellion? Or will you make a decision to take the high road – the high road of blessing and integrity? The difficult road is the one on which you have to take command of your flesh, contain your own disappointment at what you see, and honor the man of God anyway.

Turn Away

Sons, turn your face away from your father's nakedness! Show godly character in the difficult position in which you find yourself. Like Shem and Japheth, turn away from his nakedness and refuse to make it the point of focus.

Notice that when Ham went outside to announce the news to his brothers, they did not join in with him to discuss and mull over their father's bad behavior. Instead, they turned their heads when they went into the tent and would not look on. They covered their father. Decide today to cover your father's nakedness and bring Almighty God's favor down on your life. Understand this, it's not about the facts or about being right, it's all about *your heart attitude*.

Don't Kick Him When He's Down

Some sons kick their fathers when the fathers are unable to defend themselves. I want to say it again. There are times when your father is going to disappoint you, he'll disappoint God, he'll disappoint his church, and he'll disappoint his friends as well. You dare not take hold of these things as opportunities to use his nakedness to bring him down. That, my friend, is inexcusable behavior and there are many who will look back shamefully and wish they hadn't done that. God is not pleased when sons expose their father's nakedness. If you're somehow involved in that kind of thing, get out of it now. Satan is setting you up, and you stand the chance of losing your destiny in God by bringing a curse on yourself.

Everything will be Revealed

So Noah awoke from his wine, and knew what his younger son had done to him. Then he said: "Cursed be Canaan; a servant of servants he shall be to his brethren." And he said: "Blessed be the LORD, the God of Shem, and may Canaan be his servant. May God enlarge Japheth, and may he dwell in the tents of Shem; and may Canaan be his servant" (Genesis 9:24-27).

Know this, the day of reckoning is coming, and there will be a very clear accountability for our actions.

Ham thought that his father was too drunk to know or recall what had happened, but he was wrong. His father knew very well what Ham had done and was very angry. As a result, Ham was cursed by his father. He cursed him by simply withdrawing his inheritance and giving it all to the sons who had shown him honor in his moment of vulnerability.

Act with Honor

Another question is, where were you when your father needed you to cover his nakedness? As with Noah, he will wake up in the morning and will be himself again. He will come through the drunkenness, clothe himself, and walk out of his tent once again as the man of authority.

Will you be able to look him in the eye and be satisfied in your heart that you have treated him with honor? Did you protect him and cover his nakedness when he couldn't do it himself? Will you experience camaraderie with your brothers who wouldn't look on his nakedness and who pulled the blanket over him?

Fathers will become naked. There is no doubt about this. It is only a matter of time before the wine from the vine takes effect. Will the details of their uncovering become public or a talking point? If so, will that happen because of your actions—will you be like Ham?

Have you been involved in this type of thing? Well, repentance is the key to restoration. You will need restoration in your heart and restoration in your relationship with your father. If you need to, pray this prayer with me.

Father God, I come to you in the Name of Jesus.

I wish to confess that I have sinned before you and before my spiritual father. I have been privileged to be in my father's presence at all times, even when he has been naked.

When I became offended in my heart, I abused this privilege. I looked on his nakedness with disdain. I exposed his nakedness and abused my position of trust. I have spoken out about these things instead of covering my father's nakedness. I have offended You, and I'm sorry. Please forgive me for this sin and release me from the load I now bear.

Furthermore, I choose to release my spiritual father to be naked from time to time as he partakes of the vine.

Thank You, Lord.

Amen.

Thank you for being sincere. It is now in your power to go to your father and repair the relationship. It is also in your power to help those who are caught up in the practice of abusing their father's nakedness.

Chapter 7

Jabez

Now Jabez was more honorable than his brothers, and his mother called his name Jabez, saying, "Because I bore him in pain." And Jabez called on the God of Israel saying, "Oh, that You would bless me indeed, and enlarge my territory, that Your hand would be with me, and that You would keep me from evil, that I may not cause pain!" So God granted him what he requested (1 Chronicles 4:9-10).

I am absolutely sold on the prayer of Jabez. When I first encountered the prayer I was mesmerized. Everything that I've always believed about the character of God was confirmed in my heart the day that I read about Jabez and how God answered his prayer. I am still mesmerized.

I've read it and studied it so many times. This prayer and the account of Jabez has become revelation to me over and over again. I've taught the revelation to my church with passion. I've even named my boat "Jabez' Prayer."

God's Favor

Jabez found God's favor, in part, by praying this simple prayer.

"Oh, that You would bless me indeed, and enlarge my territory, that Your hand would be with me, and that You would keep me from evil, that I may not cause pain!"

I have seen God's great favor on my life as I've prayed the prayer of Jabez in faith. God gave me a house. I mean that literally; He ***gave*** me the house I now own. I live in a very expensive part of our country, in a town called Knysna, on the Garden Route, on the south coast of South Africa. Property is very expensive here, and I believe that our area is known as one of the premier real estate investments in the world today. A man walked into our home one Tuesday morning and gave us a check as a gift. He said it was from God the Father. It was to buy a house. The check was enough for us to buy the house we were renting in cash. Since we have planted our church we have been given five cars including a late model BMW that I now drive. The blessings are too many to list here. I'd like to spend a lot more time on the subject, but there's something else I wish to emphasize.

We all want Blessings

Every one of us wants what Jabez wanted. We all want to receive what he received.

He asked to be blessed, and God blessed him.

He asked God to enlarge his territory, and it was done for him.

He asked for God's hand to be with him, and it was granted.

Sons, do you desire God's blessing on your lives? Do you want God's best? Do you want to prosper greatly in every area of your lives—especially in the realm of your destinies?

If so, then let's have a brief look at some of the things that set Jabez apart from others. I've learned that the men and women who actually see their destiny in God fulfilled in their lifetimes are those who stand apart from others. You cannot be "Mr. Average" and expect to go far. You must accept that there are things about you that are going to have to set you apart from mediocrity. The path of least resistance is the wrong route for you to take if you wish to fulfill the holy calling that God has placed upon your life.

Get ready for change.

All Truth is Parallel

There is a concept in God's kingdom that every Christian would do well to embrace. It is this—***all truth is parallel***. It means that one truth in God's kingdom is not more important than other truths. It's like a train that needs both tracks on which to run.

For instance, I preach very strongly on the grace of God. I teach that we are the righteousness of God in Christ Jesus. We are saved by grace and not by works. This is true, and people typically respond very excitedly to this message. However, I must be careful to preach the *whole* gospel. So, I also preach that faith without works is dead, and that God will judge sin. On the one hand, we are saved by grace and walk by grace, but if we choose to sin, we will bear the consequences of our actions. People are typically much quieter when I preach the latter. The point I'm making is that all truth is on an equal plain of importance. We will fail God if we only teach our people the things that make them *feel* good.

Don't Polarize!

Some people polarize. That means that they begin to believe that their pet doctrine will sort out any need that people have. They believe that their revelation is *the* revelation! They think that somehow their concept, specialized teaching, or ministry is God's answer to all the needs of the world. They come to think that all other ministries are lacking if *their* teaching is not included.

For example, some folk just want to cast out demons. If there is a problem, cast a demon out! Call the deliverance ministry, and it will all be fixed. Other people only want to minister about money, blessing, and prosperity. People love to hear sermons that will help them get more money, more blessings, and more prosperity. Everyone wants to be blessed. Ever wonder why folk that only preach about how to get blessed never mention that Paul also taught us that it's OK to go without sometimes? For instance, he was happy whether he had a lot or a little. The reason that many "prosperity preachers" do not speak about the whole truth is that it isn't what people actually want to hear. Who's going to come to hear sermons on how to get blessed, if they're going to have to face the cold reality of all facets of the gospel including the idea of being grateful for what one has, even if it is a little? I believe in, and preach very confidently on, God's prosperity for His people, but I've come to learn that, if we want God's full blessing in life, we have to embrace God's full truth, even the parts that don't make us feel good.

I know how to be abased, and I know how to abound. Everywhere and in all things I have learned both to be full and to be hungry, both to abound and to suffer need (Philippians 4:12).

Preachers often fall into the trap of making their sermons and teachings as attractive and popular as possible. They don't actually lie, they simply leave out some of the truth.

So, there are various reasons why people polarize on one particular truth. There are also various reasons why people polarize on one particular presentation of the truth. There are even various reasons why people polarize on one selected angle of the truth. People tend to gravitate toward things that sound comfortable and that promise gain in some form. This approach to the gospel can become a value and a lifestyle. This means that they see through the reading glasses of their comfort zones. What they see is actually distorted.

Remember, we shouldn't alter our theology to fit the way we think, but we should alter our thinking to be obedient to theology. (Don't be put off by that word "theology"—it means the study of God).

So, Why was Jabez Blessed?

Let me share some truths about Jabez. There are principles in the account of Jabez that have a direct bearing on what I'm teaching here. Most of us would be very happy to embrace the parts that promise us blessing and prosperity. This approach is incorrect. You see, if we're in the habit of polarizing on the doctrines or values that we favor, polarizing becomes a life pattern, and we begin to see scripture the way that we prefer it to look. We begin to hear and see selectively. We don't get the complete picture so we miss what God is saying. We can become polarized in our doctrine and actually begin to subconsciously reject scripture that contradicts our pre-conceived and incorrect definitions of truth. Or we may begin to divide scripture and put aside anything that costs a price to obey. This is how a person who is polarized toward only looking for an easy blessing will read the scripture containing the prayer of Jabez.

*Now Jabez was more honorable than his brothers, and his mother called his name Jabez, saying, "Because I bore him in pain." **And Jabez called on the God of Israel saying, "Oh, that You would bless me indeed, and enlarge my territory, that Your hand would be with me**, and that You would keep me from evil, that I may not cause pain!" **So God granted him what he requested** (1 Chronicles 4:9-10).

The parts of the scripture in bold are the parts that sound exciting and give promise of blessing and gain. These are the words that we easily grab hold of and remember. They get into our memory, and we learn to confess and quote them excitedly in an attitude of faith.

The words not in bold are the words that spell out the price that Jabez paid to see God's blessing manifested in his life. These are the words that we skim over quickly when we're reading or studying. These are thoughts and truths on which we tend *not* to spend time.

Sons in the house, God wants to pour out His full portion of goodness in your lives. It is His plan to take you on to great things in Him. Your destiny and calling are uppermost in His mind. Be assured, if you honor God with obedience, He will bring you to a place of glory that only He can bring you to.

I would like to highlight some of the less obvious values that Jabez lived and prayed to secure the blessing of God. Be prepared to grab hold of these truths. They are uncomfortable to live out but key to your blessing and destiny.

Honor

Now Jabez was more honorable than his brothers (1 Chronicles 4:9a).

This is the foundation on which the whole "Jabez experience" is built. He had more **honor** than his brothers. He lived more honorably than all the other sons. This was very important. If it were not so, then the Holy Spirit would not have ensured that it was recorded in the Scriptures. Jabez was the most upright of all the sons in his family. There was something about him that set him apart and gave him a place of honor. This is what you have to do. You must make the decision to take your eyes off of others and what they're doing. Don't be a crowd pleaser or a crowd follower. What's *in* is not always what's *right*. What's *comfortable* isn't always what's *acceptable*.

Low Road or High Road?

You will always have those around you who will act less honorably than they ought. There are many who take the low road. The path of least resistance is always the most popular. It takes an unusual kind of dedication to righteousness to stick to the values that you know in your heart are correct. Make a decision to be different. Be a good son in the house. Listen to what the Holy Spirit is saying to you as you read this book. The things that I'm imparting to you aren't just things that I've read or heard somewhere. I'm talking about powerful principles that the Lord has taught me and that I live by. Sometimes the lessons that I've learned have been painful. They didn't have to be. So save yourself some pain and don't repeat some of the mistakes that I've made. On the other hand, I've done some good, sensible things as well. I've been blessed to have heard the voice of God early in my life, and I also made the right decisions at that time.

I decided a long time ago to be different and to break away from the crowd and the flow of popular behavior. I chose to obey God and be a good son. I chose to be more honorable than my brothers in the house. Please don't think that I'm pretending to be better than others. I certainly do not think that I'm some superior person or that I'm better than my peers. I am merely trying to share real life experiences with you. I paid a high price to be a good son in the house in which God placed me. It wasn't easy to choose the high road in the house, but I did, and I have seen God reward me with more than I deserve.

You know something? I've never really struggled in the ministry. It's a funny thing. I meet with many pastors and others in the ministry, and we talk. I hear some really "hard luck" stories of people in the ministry who have had such a bad time or where the going was really tough. In contrast, I've always won the battles that I've been through in the ministry. Our church has been blessed financially. We've seen awesome growth and have made tremendous strides in positively affecting our community with the gospel. I believe that I am now reaping all that I have sown as a son. I chose to be "more honorable than my brothers," and I am now seeing the fruit.

To Not Cause Pain

And that You would keep me from evil, that I may not cause pain! (1 Chronicles 4:10b)

Jabez had something big in his favor. He knew how to please God. He also knew what would block the flow of God's blessing. He understood that it was equally important to get his own house in order in preparation for his petition for God's blessing.

We Are All Born in Pain

I would like to backtrack a little bit to emphasize something about you that you may have never thought about. Of course, this is a truth about me as well, and also about every believer in God's kingdom.

You and I were born in pain. Our birth and our entry into this world caused pain. Others endured pain so that we could live.

His mother called his name Jabez, saying, "Because I bore him in pain" (1 Chronicles 4:9b).

This phrase, "*Because I bore him in pain*" holds special significance, and I would like to explore this concept.

Every child born into this world is born in pain. The degree of pain will vary, but the presence of pain in birth is an accepted fact. It's a part of life, and that's that. We can deny it and maybe even pretend that it isn't so, but that won't change the reality of life. The birth of children into this world is done in pain. Anyone who has been around for a while will be familiar with the agonizing screams of mothers as they labor and give those final pushes to bring a new baby into this world. We have images of women with contorted faces experiencing a great deal of anxiety, brows glistening with perspiration until the baby arrives.

So it is spiritually. The birth of new Christians is accompanied with pain. This is also a fact of life in the church. Not one newborn Christian experienced the new birth without someone else bearing pain. We must not take our salvation lightly. Someone paid with the burden of intercessory prayer. Someone put up with our bad attitudes in order to get close enough to us to bring us to Jesus.

A Price to Pay

After the birth itself, the first years of rearing children are also done with pain. It is a different type of pain, but it is pain nevertheless. There is nothing in this world that can prepare a husband and wife for the arrival of a new addition to the family. The degree of responsibility that is demanded of them from the moment that little child is born is totally consuming. Their whole lives become subject to the needs of the baby. Some women experience post-natal depression as the sheer enormity of the situation envelops them. Other parents enter a state of panic as they realize that there is now a little helpless person that requires their focus every minute of every hour of every day of every week of every month without a break. This is a phenomenal adjustment to life and a completely new lifestyle. While the presence of new babies brings much joy, the parents pay a great price to have them. This is part of that pain.

I have 3 young children—all girls. In each instance, the first two or three years of parenthood, although filled with great happiness, also brought their share of pain.

Young children can't help themselves. They cause a lot of problems just because they're there. This experience is constant in all families and should be calculated into the equation when expecting new children.

Make no mistake, I wouldn't change or swap any of my girls for the world. My wife and I have no regrets, and I'm sure that any parent reading this will agree with me. It is part of the family experience that these children, whom we love so much, will do things that are going to cost us. Once they come along, life changes.

The other day I noticed that the rug under the coffee table in the lounge had a new bright blue paint spill that was really obvious. On closer examination, I realized that this paint mark on the carpet was fresh and that it was permanent. It was probably Casey, the eight-year-old, who is always drawing, painting, and being creative. What could I do about it? Nothing, really. It's done now and cannot be undone. I've come to terms with this kind of thing. It's one small example of pain.

The other day, Jenna, the little one, was teething. She's such a beautiful little thing with a happy, lovable character. She's a shining star filled with joy. Jenna is simply gorgeous, and I would die for her. She became really sick through the teething process. She had diarrhea, couldn't keep anything down, and was moaning from nausea. I empathized with her and was even angry because she was so sick. My heart felt broken as I watched her have such a difficult time.

This is pain. It is part of the price I and her mother pay to bring her to adulthood. I think you will understand what I'm talking about. The stories that I can tell to illustrate my point are as numerous as there are days. The very presence of growing youngsters is a source of pain to those around them.

The parallel is evident in God's kingdom. The fathering and discipling of every new and young believer in our ministry is a source of joy and a source of pain at the same time.

Please don't misunderstand me here. There are no regrets. I wouldn't have it any other way. Neither would my parents, nor theirs. I'm not in any way griping about the pain I bear to rear my girls. I'm not griping about the price I pay to raise young believers to maturity. I'm exposing a very pertinent factor in the story of life itself. I have counted the cost and have made my decisions. I'm here for the long haul regardless of the price involved.

I want you to see what it costs for your salvation and the support structure that has gone into raising you up in the things of God.

Jabez was indeed born in pain, just like the rest of us.

Growing Up

That I may not cause pain! (1 Chronicles 4:10b)

Jabez knew that his beginning had been clothed in pain—the pain of those who were responsible for him when he was helpless. He was greatly moved. He accepted that there was nothing he could do about the past, but he decided positively, with conviction, that there was a whole lot that he could do about the present and the future.

As we grow in the house, there comes a time that we no longer ought to be causing the pain that we used to as young Christians. It is sad to see a grown man still sucking a spiritual pacifier and acting like a spiritual baby, making messes everywhere.

Jabez prayed that God would help him no longer cause pain as he did before. What a great insight he had. Sons, I pray that God gives you the discernment to understand what is being said and the character to live accordingly. You need to mature spiritually to the point that you no longer cause pain to your spiritual father or family. This principle is a powerful foundation on which to build your destiny. It is a decision with corresponding action that will have long, far-reaching, positive consequences for you. Decide that you will no longer be a causer of pain.

Sons Who Cause Pain

Many sons enter realms of evil when they are caught up by and seduced into betrayal and rebellion against their fathers. These actions always cause pain, sometimes producing great heartache for their fathers. Sons who have rejected the fathering that I've offered have caused me tremendous anguish. Every spiritual father will be able to tell vivid stories of how some have caused them great pain.

I have seen the hurt and the heartache in the eyes of fathers who have been deeply wounded by sons who cause pain. I'm not talking about "the pain of the process." I'm talking about the ugly kind of pain that is caused when sons are grown up and purposefully set out to hurt their fathers and brothers. I have often detected loneliness in these fathers—a loneliness that comes from too many betrayals. Often, fathers enter into a realm of self-preservation and begin to withdraw. They don't allow sons too close to them so that when the pain does come, it will not affect them that much. This may not be right, but sons must do their share so that they don't become part of the problem.

Sometimes sons have the attitude that, no matter how long the duration and how much pain they cause, the fathers must be superspiritual beings and not feel anything.

We must look at our actions and be objective. Have we been causing pain? Are we in the habit of doing so and justifying our actions because we are focused on our own wants and desires and aren't even aware that we are hurting others in the process? We need to mature beyond making excuses for our actions. Stop causing pain and become accountable to God. Otherwise, the enemy will steal your inheritance.

This Ought Not To Be

On March 5, 2002, I experienced a violent and extremely dangerous heart attack. In fact, I had more than one heart attack that day and the doctors did not give me much chance of surviving. I was rushed to Bayview Hospital in Mossel Bay, South Africa. I was in deep trouble, but much prayer was offered on my behalf. There were people all over the world who were praying for me. At about 7:00 that evening, I died just after I had an angiogram. My heart stopped after another attack, and I "flat-lined" as my blood pressure plummeted to zero. I was rushed into theatre where they opened my chest and connected me to the bypass machine.(I don't know all the medical terms, but I'm trying my best.) I regained consciousness at 1:00 the next afternoon after a harrowing night for my wife, my congregation, and my friends. My survival was a miracle. I was in the intensive care unit for 7 days. I had had quadruple heart bypass surgery and was now recovering. I have simplified this testimony, but in fact, I felt as if I'd been to hell and back again, not to mention the trauma that my family had also experienced. At the time, my youngest daughter, Jenna, was only two weeks old.

When I got home I could hardly walk and was in a great deal of pain and discomfort. I couldn't even pick up a loaf of bread. The worst part of the ordeal was the emotional trauma. I was a broken man. I had no idea why this had happened. The doctors were surprised because I was physically fit and not a typical candidate for a heart attack. I had a major fight on my hands to try to regain my confidence and the ability to see beyond the immediate future. Emotionally, I was in a bad way. I would broke down and began to cry at any time. The tears would well up from nowhere, and I'd groan from the inner pain of my traumatic experience. It was the most difficult time of my life.

In the midst of this, three days after my release from intensive care, a man and his wife walked into my house. This man had been a friend of mine. We got on well together. We played squash and spent time talking with each other. However, our friendship turned out to be a lie. He and his wife had pledged their commitment and trust, and I had been conned. I was in a great deal of emotional shock when this man arrived at my home. He had been offended somehow and launched a verbal attack on me that completely broke my heart. There was no mention of "How're you doing?" or "I'm standing with you" or anything similar. I remember that I was dressed in a nightgown, hardly able to stand up and holding on to a cupboard in the kitchen. I was weak and defenseless.

I had trusted them, but during this confrontation, I realized that everything that they had presented to me had been false. This all occurred right in the middle of the hardest time of my life, while I was literally fighting for my survival. To this day, I have no idea what had offended that couple. I later found out that they had made malicious accusations against me. I had been blessed by God, and I was able to buy a boat. This man told the story that I'd purchased the boat using church funds. He also spread other dangerous lies. He tried to cause disunity in our church and destroy my ministry even as I lay fighting for my life.

I am not relating this incident to cause anyone to feel sorry for me. I have recovered from the heart attacks, am back in the saddle, and am feeling fit emotionally. The reason that I'm giving this testimony is to point out how hurtful and painful sons' actions can be. This man dealt me the lowest blow that I've ever received in all of my years in the ministry. The betrayal was completely devastating. It took me a long time to get over that one. He kicked me when I was down and then kicked me some more. Although I was able to recover from this experience because of the anointing and love of God, I do believe that this man will be held accountable for his actions. He may have left our church, but that is not the end of it. He will still have to bear the consequences of his sin before God.

Taking Responsibility

Sons, I urge you to consider your actions. Are you causing pain? Are those around you causing pain? Rise up and do something about it. Be big!

Jabez asked God to keep him from evil and not to let him cause pain. Sons, make this your prayer as much as you pray for the blessing. Pray that God keeps you from evil. This means to keep you from doing evil. Also pray that God keeps you from causing pain. I have given you an example of a brother who caused great pain and, in so doing, found himself *doing* evil. Don't you fall into the same snare.

Jabez asked for God's blessing, and he also asked God to enlarge his territory. But Jabez had a clear understanding of those things that would be a righteous foundation on which to build. In other words, he knew to put *first things first*.

Rather than only petitioning God's blessing, Jabez had a deep desire to walk uprightly. He wasn't polarized toward the blessing, but instead welcomed his own responsibility in the relationship. He understood that the train had to ride on both tracks.

Don't allow yourself to be used by the devil to cause pain. If you allow this, you may find yourself being used as a weapon in the hands of satan against God's people.

In the house, determine to be more honorable than your brothers. Ask and expect God to bless you and to enlarge your territory as you seek to refrain from evil and from causing pain, especially toward your spiritual father. The blessings will overtake you. The blessing and enlarging of your territory is relevant to your destiny and calling. You need God's blessing and you need God to enlarge your territory. However, you must walk in honor, keep from evil, and refrain from causing pain in order to receive God's blessing.

If you've been the causer of pain, repent today. This is very important.

If you're about to, or are in the process of, causing pain, cease immediately and withdraw from that action.

If you're associating closely with people who are causing pain, withdraw from that relationship until they've sorted their hearts out. Don't allow their offence and anger to come upon you and to ensnare you by the spirit that drives their hearts.

Once you've gotten your priorities straight and your foundations in order and you understand and accept these changes in your thinking, you are ready to pray the entire prayer of Jabez.

Now Jabez was more honorable than his brothers, and his mother called his name Jabez, saying, "Because I bore him in pain." And Jabez called on the God of Israel saying, "Oh, that You would bless me indeed, and enlarge my territory, that Your hand would be with me, and that You would keep me from evil, that I may not cause pain!" So God granted him what he requested (1 Chronicles 4:9-10).

Chapter 8

The Threshing Floor

His winnowing fan is in His hand, and He will thoroughly clean out His threshing floor, and gather His wheat into the barn; but He will burn up the chaff with unquenchable fire (Matthew 3:12).

I'm amazed at how the Holy Spirit will say so much in so few words. This little, seemingly insignificant verse communicates a wealth of wisdom and revelation in the things of God. We see the whole concept of discipleship in the local church unveiled in a short sentence. Entire books could be written and many, many sermons preached from just these few words.

Allow me to explain the terms and culture of the times referred to in this verse.

At harvest time, the wheat was reaped by using the sickle and was into sheaves. Harvest time was a season of great joy and happiness, accentuated by many celebrations and festivals.

The threshing floor was usually a cleared area of pounded, hardened ground or a large flat rock where the wheat was brought for threshing. It was typically situated on the outskirts of a village in order to take advantage of the prevailing winds.

The process of threshing involved removing the kernels of grain from the waste straw or chaff. The wheat was placed on the threshing floor in thick layers. For small amounts of wheat, the farmers would beat the grain or have their animals with specially shod hooves walk to and fro over the wheat.

When there was a lot more wheat to be threshed, a different method was used. They would use a "threshing sledge." The threshing sledge was animal drawn and made of planks with rocks, pieces of metal, or other forms of roughage attached underneath. The farmer would have his animals pull this contraption back and forth over the wheat on the threshing floor. Sometimes, to add more weight, the farmer would place rocks or seat his family on top of the threshing sledge.

Once the wheat had been threshed, the farmer would use the winnowing fork or fan. The winnowing fan is actually a pitchfork with a long handle. He would thrust the fork into the threshed wheat and toss it into the air numerous times. The wind would blow through the wheat and carry the chaff away. The heavier kernels would fall to the ground, and the farmer would collect them for removal to the barn.

The Holy Spirit revealed to me that the account and experiences of my life as a son in the house are summarized in this illustration. This applies to all believers who are in earnest pursuit of God, and I therefore feel it is important that I share my experiences and my own revelation from the Holy Spirit with you.

Harvest

The harvest in the fields represents all the un-reached and unsaved masses.

Then He said to them, "The harvest truly is great, but the laborers are few; therefore pray the Lord of the harvest to send out laborers into His harvest" (Luke 10:2).

I was one of those in the field. Then, a harvester, sent by the Lord of the harvest, came and harvested me. There was great celebration and joy at my salvation. There were many who celebrated with great relief when I finally repented and turned from a life of self-destruction to a life of serving Jesus Christ.

When I was saved and came into the kingdom I became so aware of all the happiness around me. I remember the euphoria caused by my salvation and how everything was just wonderful. My deliverance from drugs and all that goes with that lifestyle was quite dramatic. My new-found acceptance and joy in Jesus had me floating on air. My joy was immeasurable and complete.

The Local Church – The Threshing Floor

Immediately after my conversion I found myself in the local church. It was all so new and exciting. Nothing could keep me from church. At church, I felt as though I were walking on air. To me, it was the ultimate romance. I lived from meeting to meeting. It was an awesome time for me. Whenever I think back on that time in my life, it always brings a smile to my face and joy to my heart.

A season went by and things were no longer as simple and uncomplicated as they were initially. I found that there was an increasing pressure brought to bear on me as the Holy Spirit focused on heart and character issues in my life. All this happened in the local church. This process became increasingly offensive to me. I had always been incredibly independent and was used to having my own way. I was very young when I left home and joined the army. Even the army could not bring me under control and now I was suddenly faced with accountability and structure in the very place in which I had recently found so much freedom.

Do you know what? I was on the threshing floor. Yessir! I found myself on God's threshing floor. Over the years, I've become convinced that the local church is God's threshing floor. All the wheat that comes from the field must go onto the threshing floor where it can be prepared and made ready for the Master's use.

No Shortcuts

Sons, the threshing floor is probably the most important preparation process that you'll experience on your way to spiritual adulthood. It's also probably the most painful and difficult process. So many disciples don't understand or embrace this vital part of their lives as Christians, which results in failure to reach their true potential.

I recognize this process because I've experienced it. Therefore, I also identify with the pain that the sons in my house go through as they're brought onto the threshing floor and prepared for the Master's use. I also realize that I am an instrument in God's hands. He uses me to thresh the wheat in the local church. Sometimes I don't like my job, but I've seen so many sons go into spiritual adulthood and fail because they've been allowed to escape the "threshing floor" process. Therefore, I dare not back down from my responsibility as a spiritual father. It is very difficult for me to watch those whom I love so much being crushed and sifted on the threshing floor. However, for their own sakes, I must persevere with them as a good father. It is distressing for me to see them battle with issues that they sometimes do not comprehend. The best I can do is help them through, and I'm convinced that there is no shortcut or by-passing of the process.

His winnowing fan is in His hand, and He will thoroughly clean out His threshing floor... (Matthew 3:12a).

I can imagine Jesus standing there beside the threshing floor, leaning on His winnowing fork while watching the threshing of the wheat with expectancy.

Remember that the threshing occurs to separate the kernel of the grain from the waste, stalk, or chaff.

Wrestling

When all the euphoria of my salvation began to subside, I found myself in a spiritual wrestling match as I struggled to let go of the things that gave me security in my old life. These things are represented by the straw, stalks, and chaff that the threshing process had to break up on the threshing floor. I began to experience strain as the threshing started. In fact, my independence and rebellion threatened to draw me away.

I thought, "I don't need this." I was ruled by the independent spirit to which I had given myself over. I never trusted anyone, and I absolutely hated being told what to do. I also suffered from major rejection issues from which the threshing had to loosen me.

In addition, my volatile temper and violent manifestations had to be threshed out. I was self-opinionated and headstrong, quick to get into confrontation and cause strife. Boy, when I think back, I feel really sorry for my spiritual father who was the one who had to walk me through the threshing floor. I am also grateful that he never gave up on me. (Thank you, Pastor Jimmy.) The fact is, if all these things that were chaff in my life were pointed out to me when I first came in from the harvest field, I would not have believed them. Thank God for the local church. Thank God for the threshing floor.

When I first perceived the concept of relating the threshing floor to the local church, my immediate response was negative. I thought that I'd misunderstood what the Holy Spirit was trying to say but He persevered with me. The reason that I almost rejected the idea was because of the way in which the wheat was threshed. It seemed pretty violent to say the least - all that crushing and ripping and tearing. How could I compare what happened to the wheat on the threshing floor to the threshing of the sons on the floor of the local church? As I meditated on this, I began to understand.

The process of threshing the wheat by the thresher was not designed or planned to crush and *destroy* the wheat, but rather to *separate* the wheat from the parts that are unusable. The Master is not able to use wheat that is full of sticks, straw, and chaff.

Certainly there is a crushing that comes later, but the rubbish must first be removed because, once the wheat is crushed with the chaff, the chaff can no longer be removed.

Everything had to be loosened prior to the next level of preparation by the Master. So, the threshing on the threshing floor of the local church was intense, thorough, and sometimes very, very uncomfortable.

We must remember that this process is for our good. It is not to destroy us but to separate us from all those things that so easily beset us as sons in the house.

Come, Holy Spirit

When the process of threshing was complete, the farmer would then put in the winnowing fork. He would then scoop the wheat and fling it into the air. As the wind blew through it all, the heavier kernels of wheat fell to the ground, and the wind blew everything away that was now loosened and broken up.

The wind is the Holy Spirit. He will begin to blow through your life. As the wind of the Spirit comes, He will pick up whatever you've allowed to be loosened. He will continue blowing. This process can take many years. For some, it will not even reach completion in their lifetime.

As the farmer performed his task, he would throw the wheat into the air a few times and then stoop down to examine the improvement. He would be looking to see how much of the waste was, in fact, blown away and how much of what was left still had to be removed. He would only be satisfied when the wheat was free of all the chaff. He would keep throwing it up in the air with the winnowing fork until he was satisfied.

Take note. The winnowing fork is in Jesus' hand. He is the one who's throwing the wheat into the air. You're the wheat; He's the thrower. I believe that the winnowing fan is your spiritual father in the house. Therefore, your spiritual father is also in Jesus' hands.

Very often, sons become confused and begin to blame their fathers when they have a tough time.

Those times, when everything seems so out of control and confusing, are the times when the sons are in the air, with the wind of the Holy Spirit blowing through their lives. My sons have come to me saying, "Pastor, I don't know what's going on! It seems as though I'm not connecting. Where's God? Why don't I hear Him anymore? Does He even care?"

I had an impression once of a person hanging in the air as Jesus threw him up with the winnowing fork. The son was up in the air with arms and legs flailing, wide-eyed with a puzzled look on his face. His hair was blown backwards, and his clothes were flapping noisily as the sound of the rushing wind of the Spirit overwhelmed his voice. His lips mouthed silent, desperate questions.

I remember clearly. I laughed as I saw myself. Yes, that was me. I came to understand those times and even embrace them because I knew that the Spirit was dealing with issues in my life. I learned to ask the right question. "Holy Spirit, what is it that you want me to let go of?"

I see the Lord with the winnowing fork in His hand. He throws the wheat into the air. The wind blows, and the Lord waits. The wheat lands on the threshing floor again. The Lord looks down. Nope. There's still chaff that must go. In with the winnowing fork again and up into the air with the wheat. This process continues until all the chaff and waste products are removed.

When the wheat is cleaned out and all that is left after the wind has done its work are the kernels, the Lord will remove the wheat to the barn, where it is then processed. It is pure and ready for the Master's use.

I soon realized that the quicker I let go of the junk and let the wind of the Spirit blow it out of my life, the quicker I'll be ready to leave the threshing floor and be ready for the Master's use.

Stubborn Sons

Some sons remain stubborn. When they're in the local church and the Lord begins His work, using the fathers, they doggedly refuse the dealings of God. These sons try to escape the threshing floor process. Most decide to leave the house, falsely believing that, if they go elsewhere, the threshing will cease. Others stay away from the local church completely. They form little groups because, in their own deceived minds, they're right. They get themselves little platforms to air their independent opinions.

Others go for the "gypsy Christian" option. They run to this conference, that concert, this seminar, that special meeting, this guest speaker, that teacher, this prophet, etc. Similarly, others become spiritual nomads. They go from one church to the other. They never quite allow themselves to be counted faithful in the house over any substantial period of time. They move on before they become too accountable. Then there are those who sit in the local church and disconnect. They don't partake, help, or submit.

I've yet to meet a Christian in any of the above groups who is happy and satisfied. All of these Christians who have escaped the threshing floor are inwardly unhappy, unfulfilled, and empty. Most of them are angry and filled with bitterness, defiling everything with which they come into contact. This might sound exaggerated, but it is the truth.

Looking carefully lest anyone fall short of the grace of God; lest any root of bitterness springing up cause trouble, and by this many become defiled (Hebrews 12:15).

I found out that God will work with us as long as we submit to His dealings. He will go even further and call us into His plan when we rebel, but He will not pursue us indefinitely. If we are determined to escape His dealings, we will succeed in doing so.

Woe to him who strives with his Maker! Let the potsherd strive with the potsherds of the earth! Shall the clay say to him who forms it, 'What are you making?' Or shall your handiwork say, 'He has no hands'? (Isaiah 45:9)

And the LORD said, "My Spirit shall not strive with man forever, for he is indeed flesh; yet his days shall be one hundred and twenty years" (Genesis 6:3).

The Unfathered

God will not push the issue with anyone forever. There will come a time when He will see a man's or woman's refusal to allow the processes of the threshing floor refine them, and God will let them follow their own devices.

Sons, when you see others apparently getting away with this, don't fret. I know how that feels. I have seen many Christians take shortcuts to avoid God's dealings. I often wondered why I had to endure what I did when others seemed to wangle their way out and even appeared to get away with it. Today I see that they didn't get away with it at all. Their character let them down.

It is obvious that these individuals were never fathered. They are grain that is still full of chaff. These are the people whom you find everywhere who have such an awesome knowledge of how Christians should live. They are always correcting others, but their own lives fall far short of acceptable. The Bible calls this a "form of godliness but denying the power thereof." In other words, they're experts at knowing what useful and prepared wheat should look like, but they themselves are not, nor have ever been, on the threshing floor of God.

Would you be happy if you bought a loaf of fresh bread at the local bakery, and, when you sliced it, you found all sorts of little sticks and husks inside? No, you wouldn't be happy at all. You'd demand quality bread that is of a decent standard. Well, why is it that people expect God to produce quality bread with wheat that is full of junk?

He will thoroughly clean out His threshing floor, and gather His wheat into the barn... (Matthew 3:12b).

The Lord is going to do a thorough work in you when you submit to His dealings. He will then gather the wheat that is good for His use into the barn. You will not go into the barn, ready for His use, until you are thoroughly cleaned.

But He will burn up the chaff with unquenchable fire (Matthew 3:12c).

As you submit to this process and allow the Holy Spirit to blow the chaff away, He will burn that chaff with unquenchable fire. That means there is complete victory over whatever it is He is dealing with in your life.

The threshing floor is an inherent and vital part of sonship.

When I meet people again whom I haven't seen for many years, it is not uncommon for them to comment on how much I've changed. I know why. It's supernatural. It was God's threshing floor that did it. My submitting to the local church as a son in the house won me the victory over seemingly impossible odds. The characteristics that were part of my makeup and that were going to destroy me have gone. They've been burnt by unquenchable fire, never again to rise from the ashes. Hallelujah!

Looking back, I feel good!

Chapter 9

The Sons and Witchcraft

PART 1 - WITCHCRAFT

Witchcraft is pure seduction. Seduction is a show of love without the truth. In other words, he will do anything that makes you feel accepted but will never give you the full truth. I refer to witchcraft as "he" because witchcraft is satan made manifest.

Witchcraft is the effort to gain control over your mind. Witchcraft is when someone attempts to seduce you into submitting to an illegitimate authority. In other words, witchcraft desires to control you. He hungers after your will. He wants to steal your ***willpower*** so that you become a reactive, predictable loser. You don't like the word loser? Do you think it's a bit strong? Well, it's a fact. If you surrender to witchcraft, you're the loser.

Witchcraft, dripping with honey, lures you into complacency and causes you to give allegiance to the wrong powers. Witchcraft instills passivity and steals your free will. He makes you into a confused blob who lacks character and who is unable to make decisions.

Witchcraft is about unauthorized control. He will look for a weakness in you, exploit it, move in, and take over, separating you from your covering and protection. Witchcraft will attack your relationship in marriage, family, church, business, government, and any other God-given authority structure. Once witchcraft penetrates your soul, he causes you to become like a predictable puppet, void of willpower and spiritual stamina.

Witchcraft will attack by using the intended victim's carnal nature. In other words, the areas that you haven't dealt with in your life become the basic building blocks with which witchcraft works. The spirit of witchcraft will examine you from head to toe to find the one thing that he can exploit to get you under his control. These weak areas are the keys that the witchcraft spirit uses to overcome your life.

Witchcraft will always approach as an angel of light. Witchcraft will never come along and say, "Hi, I'm the devil, and I'm here to lead you astray onto the wrong road that looks right but is actually a cleverly disguised path to your destruction." This spirit will blind you to danger signs, causing you to take the route that leads over a cliff edge to disaster.

Open your Heart

I suggest you pause here and open your heart to the Holy Spirit. Ask Him to give you discernment. You may be caught up in a web of witchcraft right now and not even know it. You may be involved in witchcraft and need to repent and change your heart. You may know folk close to you who are ensnared by witchcraft and need to be delivered from his hold. If that's the case, then contact them and give them this information that I'm sharing with you.

This is a vast subject; therefore, I will only share some of the strategies and seductions that witchcraft uses to attack the sons in the house.

Infiltrating

Firstly, satan manifests witchcraft to infiltrate the local church in order to bring division in the body, especially between the sons and the fathers. Satan hates it when the spirit of fathering and sonship flows in the local church. He will do all that he can to bring a wedge between the fathers and sons. He will attempt to undermine your father in your mind and elevate a counterfeit. Watch out! He will attempt to isolate you from your father so that you become an easy target for him.

Satan's desire is to neutralize the next generation of fathers. He will do this by attacking them while these same fathers are still sons. If he can cripple your soul while you're a son, you'll produce an emotionally crippled generation after you when you become a father. Broken and bitter sons become broken and bitter fathers. In turn, these broken and bitter fathers then produce more broken and bitter sons.

There is a powerful move of the Spirit of God on the hearts of sons to be the generation that makes the difference. You can be part of this awesome generation of people of God who will be a generation to interrupt the cycle of destruction that satan has planned.

The Call of the Spirit

Behold, I will send you Elijah the prophet before the coming of the great and dreadful day of the LORD. And he will turn the hearts of the fathers to the children, and the hearts of the children to their fathers, lest I come and strike the earth with a curse (Malachi 4:5-6).

With these last verses in the Old Testament, God chose to address the issue of a cycle of destruction. He made it very clear that this is a warning to the church. The prophetic voice of the Holy Spirit is going out across the earth at this time regarding the fathers' and sons' hearts being reunited with one another. We cannot ignore the issue anymore. We cannot pretend that these divisions between fathers and sons are just an accepted part of spiritual life. We must actively address these issues and deal effectively with our hearts when we find them to be out of order.

It is not normal nor is it godly, for so many sons to be angry with and offended by their fathers. It is not right that so many sons find it acceptable to walk out and rebel against their fathers when their fathers don't "toe the line" in the sons' eyes.

God has warned us that rejection of these values will bring a curse on the earth. The word "earth" in the foregoing scripture speaks of a specific, relevant land. This means that the offending individual will bring a curse onto his own land when he enters into rebellion against his spiritual father. Of course, the same will apply to fathers who reject and refuse to be fathers to their spiritual sons.

God loves us and gives this warning to us to heed the prophetic cry of the Spirit in the earth. Heed the call of the Spirit today and respond to Him positively.

If you're willing, pray this prayer right now.

Father, I come to you in the Name of Jesus. I ask you to open my eyes that I may see through the works of satan in my life. I ask you to reveal any works of witchcraft to which I have surrendered.

Lord, I ask you to reveal the truth to me by the Holy Spirit, even if it's painful. Help me to see clearly. Remove the scales from my eyes. Expose all the lies that I have believed.

Amen

The Shepherd - a Man of War!

There are a number of witchcraft spirits that attack the church. As a father and shepherd, I have made it my business to learn about these and identify them. I have become accustomed to the battle as I've realized that a shepherd is indeed a man of war as much as he is a man of peace. Any pastor worth his salt will understand of what I speak. I often find myself in the heat of battle as witchcraft spirits attempt to infiltrate my flock to devour the sheep. These witchcraft spirits specifically target the sons, desiring to instill disillusionment, rebellion, fear, insecurity, hopelessness, and dissatisfaction in their souls.

Strong and Courageous

These spirits come through the door of the church on two legs - they live in people! They don't float in through the wall or something strange like that. They need a vehicle to carry them in, and willing people are that vehicle. By this I mean those people who, knowingly or unknowingly, harbor spirits that feel "at home" living in them. I don't consider those people my enemy, but if they won't let go of the witchcraft spirits, they will have to go out the door together with them as I eject spirits of witchcraft from my fold. When the infiltration of witchcraft has come into the church family or into our personal lives, we have to be strong and courageous to discern and identify these attacks and deal with them decisively.

Many Christians and Christian leaders alike withdraw from confronting witchcraft because they are afraid. Confronting witchcraft will always cause a stir. Witchcraft responds with threats, violence, and intimidation. It attempts to cause fear by creating the false impression that it will cost too much to confront it. This causes many Christians to retreat and tolerate witchcraft in order to keep the peace. In my experience, I have found the opposite to be true. Allowing witchcraft its way in order to keep the peace will actually cost more than you can afford. Whenever I have faced witchcraft head-on, eyeball to eyeball, I have proved that, in the face of the power of the mighty Word of God, witchcraft will run every time. Passivity in the battle is the friend of the devil.

Rebellion

For rebellion is as the sin of witchcraft, and stubbornness is as iniquity and idolatry (1 Samuel 15:23a).

Witchcraft equals rebellion equals witchcraft equals rebellion. The reason this is so is because witchcraft always involves rising up against legitimate authority—either subtly or very obviously. Witchcraft is about establishing illegitimate authority. It will attempt to discredit legitimate authority, one way or another, and replace it with illegitimate and unsanctioned authority.

It will utilize any means available to coerce people to rise up and attack the appointed authority structure. The objectives are twofold. First, witchcraft seeks to bring down or bring under its control the legitimate authority. Secondly, witchcraft seeks to bring destruction to those whom it uses to achieve its goals.

PART 2 - THE SPIRIT OF KORAH

Now Korah the son of Izhar, the son of Kohath, the son of Levi, with Dathan and Abiram the sons of Eliab, and On the son of Peleth, sons of Reuben, took men; and they rose up before Moses with some of the children of Israel, two hundred and fifty leaders of the congregation, representatives of the congregation, men of renown. They gathered together against Moses and Aaron, and said to them, "You take too much upon yourselves, for all the congregation is holy, every one of them, and the LORD is among them. Why then do you exalt yourselves above the assembly of the LORD?"

So when Moses heard it, he fell on his face; and he spoke to Korah and all his company, saying, "Tomorrow morning the LORD will show who is His and who is holy, and will cause him to come near to Him. That one whom He chooses He will cause to come near to Him Do this: Take censers, Korah and all your company; put fire in them and put incense in them before the LORD tomorrow, and it shall be that the man whom the LORD chooses is the holy one. You take too much upon yourselves, you sons of Levi!"

Then Moses said to Korah, "Hear now, you sons of Levi: Is it a small thing to you that the God of Israel has separated you from the congregation of Israel, to bring you near to Himself, to do the work of the tabernacle of the LORD, and to stand before the congregation to serve them; and that He has brought you near to Himself, you and all your brethren, the sons of Levi, with you? And are you seeking the priesthood also? Therefore you and all your company are gathered together against the LORD. And what is Aaron that you complain against him?" And Moses sent to call Dathan and Abiram the sons of Eliab, but they said, "We will not come up! Is it a small thing that you have brought us up out of a land flowing with milk and honey, to kill us in the wilderness, that you should keep acting like a prince over us? Moreover you have not brought us into a land flowing with milk and honey, nor given us inheritance of fields and vineyards. Will you put out the eyes of these men? We will not come up!"

Then Moses was very angry, and said to the LORD, "Do not respect their offering. I have not taken one donkey from them, nor have I hurt one of them." And Moses said to Korah, Tomorrow, you and all your company be present before the LORD-- you and they, as well as Aaron. Let each take his censer and put incense in it, and each of you bring his censer before the LORD, two hundred and fifty censers; both you and Aaron, each with his censer." So every man took his censer, put fire in it, laid incense on it, and stood at the door of the tabernacle of meeting with Moses and Aaron. And Korah gathered all the congregation against them at the door of the tabernacle of meeting.

Then the glory of the LORD appeared to all the congregation. And the LORD spoke to Moses and Aaron, saying "Separate yourselves from among this congregation, that I may consume them in a moment." Then they fell on their faces, and said, "O God, the God of the spirits of all flesh, shall one man sin, and You be angry with all the congregation?" So the LORD spoke to Moses, saying, "Speak to the congregation, saying, 'Get away from the tents of Korah, Dathan, and Abiram.'"

Then Moses rose and went to Dathan and Abiram, and the elders of Israel followed him. And he spoke to the congregation, saying, "Depart now from the tents of these wicked men! Touch nothing of theirs, lest you be consumed in all their sins." So they got away from around the tents of Korah, Dathan, and Abiram; and Dathan and Abiram came out and stood at the door of their tents, with their wives, their sons, and their little children.

Then Moses said: "By this you shall know that the LORD has sent me to do all these works, for I have not done them of my own will. If these men die naturally like all men, or if they are visited by the common fate of all men, then the LORD has not sent me. But if the LORD creates a new thing, and the earth opens its mouth and swallows them up with all that belongs to them, and they go down alive into the pit, then you will understand that these men have rejected the LORD." Now it came to pass, as he finished speaking all these words, that the ground split apart under them, and the earth opened its mouth and swallowed them up, with their households and all the men with Korah, with all their goods. So they and all those with them went down alive into the pit; the earth closed over them, and they perished from among the congregation (Numbers 16:1-33).

The following are some brief observations and truths regarding the foregoing account.

The Spirit of Korah – Still a Factor Today

Korah was a Levite. He was also a leader. Korah fell prey to a seducing spirit. This evil spirit consumed him. I will call this spirit "the Spirit of Korah" as a point of reference.

The spirits that caused many people in the Bible to sin still live in the earth today. These spirits to whom men submitted their hearts did not die when the people died. These spirits continue to manifest in the earth in the same way as they did then. The spirits are identified by the fruits that they manifested, or by the person, nation, or place where they manifested.

The spirit that controlled and directed Korah continues to seek those who may be seduced by it. The spirit of Korah will attempt to take hold of your will and your mind so that it can lead you to the same end that Korah experienced. When the spirit manifested in Korah, it manifested clear and specific characteristics. When Korah died, that spirit (which inhabited Korah) didn't die, but he then pursued his evil desires in the next generation and so on. The spirit of Korah is alive and well today and desires to manifest his will in you, me, and every other Christian.

Be sober, be vigilant; because your adversary the devil walks about like a roaring lion, seeking whom he may devour (1 Peter 5:8).

Korah, who was a Levite, brought a company of men and challenged the authority of Moses and Aaron.

They gathered together against Moses and Aaron and said to them, "You take too much upon yourselves, for all the congregation is holy, every one of them, and the LORD is among them. Why then do you exalt yourselves above the congregation of the LORD?"

Korah – The Accuser

The spirit of Korah will speak through men and women. He will speak against God's appointed authority. The spirit of Korah will drive men with jealousy, rebellion, anger, and fear.

As recorded in the scripture, Korah makes the following accusations:

You take too much upon yourselves - you're too big for your boots and have assumed too much authority.

For all the congregation is holy, every one of them, and the LORD is among them - we're all anointed, not only you. We all have the Spirit and can hear God. God is not only with you, He's also with us. We also want a say.

Why then do you exalt yourselves above the congregation of the LORD? So why do you put yourself in charge? Who do you think you are anyway? You think you're better than the rest of us. You've placed yourself higher than us.

I have found in my own ministry and also in other ministries that every single time people rise up against local church leadership, some or all of the above accusations are leveled by the accusers. It is so predictable. Why? Because the devil does nothing new. We ought to spend more time studying Jesus and His nature than the ways of the devil. However, it is important to know your opponent. The strategies and characteristics of certain spirits that operate in the church are constant and have been so throughout the ages because they are the same spirits that have been operating against the church through the generations.

Identify the Enemy

I have spoken to many pastors who say that it seems that hell has been let loose in their ministries and they just do not know how to curb the onslaught. However, the moment the men of God are able to identify the specific spirit that is causing the attack, they are able to see the whole picture objectively and stop the enemy in his tracks. Every spirit of witchcraft has specific character traits that are always present. They all also have very predictable methods of operating.

Sons, you must not be ignorant concerning the operating strategies of the spirit of Korah. You must be able to recognize his nature the moment he shows himself so that you can take appropriate action.

Back to the scripture passage and the accusations.

How Does This Happen?

These accusations are filled with offence. Korah and his cohorts were making some wild statements against the leaders whom they once followed. Korah and his friends were not stupid people. They were men of renown. The question is, how do men of such high esteem fall so low? How do men of renown become conned into joining their hearts to such a diabolical entity as the spirit of Korah? This has puzzled me. I have seen really faithful people suddenly become offended and angry. How does this happen? How do clear thinking people get into such error? It is more conceivable that folk can become offended and angry at people they're not close to or don't even like or know. This is not too difficult for a seducing spirit of witchcraft to orchestrate. However, I have been witness to the hatred and resentment spewing from the mouths of people towards those whom they previously respected and loved. This is difficult to comprehend. I've seen sons turn against fathers with such hardness of heart that it seems almost impossible that those sons were once in that house at all!

The scary thing is that, once people have surrendered their will to a seducing spirit of any kind, it gets a hold of their mind and they begin to see error as truth. In other words, when a person is deceived by a seducing spirit, he or she has no ability to discern. It is only when these people call out to God in repentance to show them the truth that their eyes will be opened.

Some of you may even now be justifying your rebellion and your attacks against your fathers in the Lord. Ask yourself this question, "How did it all start? How did I get into this state of anger and bitterness towards my spiritual father?"

I encourage you to examine your heart carefully. Forget about whether you're right or wrong. Think about how it all started, and you'll find that you have fallen prey to seduction.

Let's examine how this spirit operates to bring an offence in your heart against your spiritual father.

This spirit is an old master at causing you to become offended and angry against the one who has cared for you and taught you regarding the things of God.

Your Mind - The Key

A few years ago my wife, Lynne, sold life insurance. The company that she worked for offered a course on the products.

During the course, they did a section on long-term and short- term goals. This course was given in a secular environment, and the lecturer was speaking from a secular, scientific point of view.

He made a startling statement. He said, "Your brain does not know the difference between fantasy and reality." This is a scientific fact, and the concept is being taught in sales and motivational conferences around the world. What he was saying was that if you can imprint a picture on your mind's eye via your imagination, your brain does not know whether that picture is coming from what your eye is actually seeing in reality or whether your eyes are closed and you're picturing something with your imagination. I do not want to enter the whole debate concerning the doctrine of visualization here, but obviously, the One who created us understands this principle.

But I say to you that whoever looks at a woman to lust for her has already committed adultery with her in his heart (Matthew 5:28).

Why did Jesus say this? He said it because He knows how we function. If a man looks at a woman and lusts after her, it means that he has fantasized about her in his thoughts. He has placed pictures of her, via his imagination, on his mind. His brain does not differentiate between reality and imagination. His body and emotions respond as though the picture were a real life experience. So, if he lusts after a woman by fantasizing about being together with her sexually, he will begin to experience all sorts of physical, sexual responses. These responses are triggered by images in his mind that are not real but that *seem* real. These real sexual feelings are what satan now uses to drag the man into a real-life sinful experience because he has already had a taste of it using his imagination. His mind perceives the fantasy as real. Likewise, your perception is truth to you whether it is real or not.

I can paint a picture on the canvas of your mind by talking about the meaty redness of a thick steak being singed to a golden brown as it is being laid on a hot grill. As it sizzles and splutters, the rich smoke rises, and the aroma of the grilled steak drifts up into your nostrils.

That is a simple illustration, but if you love steak, this will have you wanting one. Your taste buds will be *talking* to you. We respond to imaginary scenarios all the time.

A Wrong Imagination

This is how the spirits of witchcraft work. In order to get you offended at your spiritual father or anyone else, the seducing spirit will first attempt to paint a wrong picture of them on the canvas of your mind. Once you've allowed the false picture to be printed on your mind, you're an easy target for satan. Don't submit to this process. If the wrong image settles in your mind, even though it is false, you will see it as fact.

Know Your Father

Let's talk about our spiritual fathers. How many people have actually taken the time to get to **know** their spiritual fathers—who they really are. I think this is important. When I say *know*, I mean that you should have a clear picture in your mind of who they really are, including their strengths and their weaknesses. You need to establish this clearly in your heart. Don't jump to conclusions, refer to preconceived ideas, or listen to other opinions. Check it out for yourself.

A seducing spirit will attempt to depict an image of a father who is unapproachable, uncaring, bossy, false, covetous, harsh, unloving, abusive, and the list goes on. If you allow this to happen and receive that imprint on your mind, it will become a stronghold. It will become a real image even though this image is completely wrong. All that satan has to do is create an accusation. The wrong imagination in your mind is soil for the seed of accusation to germinate, grow, and produce fruit.

When you **know** your father, seducing spirits will have great difficulty selling lies to you. The truth of who your spiritual father really is will not accommodate the seed of satan.

The same principle applies in our relationship with God. I have spent many years getting to know God and His character. It will be very, very difficult for the devil to sell me a lie about God because I am absolutely certain of who He is.

For instance, if satan says to me, through people, "God is giving you a tough time. He's the one bringing sickness on you to teach you something," I would shrug that off as a lie because I know what the Bible says about God being the healer. The lie wouldn't get past first base. The image that I have in my mind of who God is has been shaped by years of experience and through study of His true character. Some unbelieving folk may come along and say, "God is the one causing lack in your life, so just be happy with suffering." I would immediately reject this because the Bible teaches me that every good and perfect gift comes from God; I have also come to know the giving nature of God experientially. I will never accept the lie that He brings lack into my life because I know Him.

See as God Sees

Determine to see your spiritual father as God sees him. When the spirit of Korah comes along with lies, you'll be armed with the correct picture of who your father is, and you won't be seduced into rebellion. Do not allow wild and unfounded imaginations and thoughts to cloud your mind. Do not entertain and nurture these vain imaginations—the Bible teaches us to cast them down!

Casting down arguments and every high thing that exalts itself against the knowledge of God, bringing every thought into captivity to the obedience of Christ (2 Corinthians 10:5).

If you don't follow this verse's instructions, the devil will paint a picture of your spiritual father that will make the next step—the accusation—acceptable. You will not accept the accusation if you hold the correct, undistorted image of your father before you. If you maintain the correct image of the father whom God has appointed in your life, the accusation that will follow will be a non-starter. It is your responsibility to keep satan out of all of the God-inspired relationships that He has put in your life.

If you've accepted the wrong image of your father and entertained those wrong thoughts and imaginations, the accusation becomes feasible to you. That "maybe" is the seed that will grow, and, before you know it, the accusation will become fact in your mind. At this point, everything that you're now believing is built on the sandy foundation of the false image that you received from satan and nurtured.

Someone may come to you and try to impart their bitterness toward your spiritual father onto you. They may bring an accusation, and that's when you need to be prepared. You need to be strong enough to say, "That can't be true. I know my father. There must be more to this story."

Broken Wings?

Witchcraft spirits will often use weak people with the "broken wing syndrome" to attack you. These people cruise around from place to place and never get their problems sorted out. They are consumers and not producers in the body. They spend all their time needing help. Their problem is not the problem concerning them. If you sort out their problem, they find another one. They will try to load their self-pity onto you and try to persuade you to take up their burden in their defense. They will go from counsel to counsel until they have exhausted all options. They will then begin to accuse people of not caring and not being there for them. Years will go by, and they will still be in the same place spiritually. I do not allow these individuals to roam endlessly around my flock. The time always comes when I will draw the line and bring them to accountability.

When this happens, they immediately begin a campaign of discrediting the body and the leadership. Sons, don't fall prey to the spirits in these people. I am glad to say that my sons in the house are well taught on these matters. When these spirits try their "stuff," I trust my sons to see through the enemy's strategies. Satan uses these people to cause major damage to the body by focusing on people in the church who are unsuspecting and who will be duped into feeling sorry for them.

One lady with the "broken wing syndrome" came into our church a few years ago, and it didn't take me long to spot the symptoms. This experience served as a learning experience for me and my church.

Every meeting, whether social or spiritual, would culminate in her being the focus of ministry input because of her "need." I mean, she would even draw all the attention at birthday parties! Soon, a number of my people were drawn into her "need." It wasn't long before many were consumed with compassion for her and wanted to come to her aid. Everyone was talking about how they could work together to bring liberty to this person. So, there was a whole lot of ministry being focused on this one "needy" soul. These people would get excited when there seemed to be a glimmer of hope that she would begin to improve. Then, just as she was at the point of recovery, she would have a relapse as some other issue arose, and everyone would be sucked into the whole process all over again.

I phoned her previous pastor, and he immediately knew what I was talking about. He called it the "listing ship" syndrome. It's as though all the cargo in a ship slides to one side and the ship lists to one side. He said that he had experienced it for eight years. Everywhere this lady went, the ship would list in her direction. Well, I was not going to have it even one week longer, so I confronted the spirit face to face. Although I have referred to her as the problem, it is very important to note that I was actually up against a wily and dangerous spirit of witchcraft that was operating through this woman.

Sure enough, when I confronted the issue, her first reaction was to break down in tears and go through the expected routine. I wasn't moved by this act of the devil. When she saw that I wasn't fazed by the bawling and self-pity, it stopped abruptly, and she launched into a violent attack about how unloving and harsh I was. The next obvious move of this spirit was to proceed rapidly through the body and try to recruit people who would carry her "burden" and side with her against the "unfeeling" and "unloving" pastor. None of these predictable actions worked, and she was gone in a few days to "ply her trade" in the church down the road.

We must be aware of the strategies of the enemy. I have trained my sons through these experiences. It is predictable that, when a person with this spirit is confronted, he or she will embark on a tearful journey through the church to get support. We can't let that stop us from doing the right thing.

Entertain Korah – Receive Offence

Satan will use every source he can find to bring accusations. Always be vigilant. Know and trust your spiritual father. When you, as a son, come to a place of discernment and you are not led astray by bewitching spirits, you're entering the realm of maturity; you're getting to a place where God can trust you.

Good sons make good fathers. Bad sons will not easily become good fathers. If you, as a son, are quick to accept accusation against your father and if you're untrusting and suspicious, you will become an accusing and suspicious father. Your accusations and suspicions will be leveled against your sons, and you will have a torrid time being a father.

Once the accusation is accepted by you, it takes root and, as you dwell on it, it produces offence and then bitterness. At this point, witchcraft has won over your mind and you're under his control. You're walking in deception and you sincerely believe that wrong is right. Bitterness is a stronghold. It must be broken.

Blinded and Bewitched

I've always been amazed when I've dealt with sons who have given themselves over to this spirit and have carried deep offence toward me. When we've sat down and spoken about it and I've confronted these spirits, I've been surprised at how these sons have completely misread me. When repentance and healing has come and these spirits have been defeated, I've heard things like, "I didn't think I could talk to you, Pastor" or "Gee Pastor, you're actually very kind and loving" or "Pastor, I'm sorry, I've completely misunderstood you. You're different from the way I saw you." "From whence" I ask, "did these misguided and false impressions of me come?"

You see, the devil bewitched these men and women when he set the stage for seduction by painting a wrong, deceptive picture of me. He was then free to bring the accusations that would cause offence and division.

People are continually being bombarded by the spirit of Korah's influence. I know who my sons are because they are the ones who will stand up to that spirit and boldly declare my character. They speak for me in my absence.

Trust Your Father

I'm very open and honest with my sons in the house. They must *trust* me. If they can't trust me, I can't father them, and they'd be better off in another church. I often have to make decisions that I do not have to explain to everyone in the church. This will be a constant for all spiritual fathers.

There have been times when I've had to exercise discipline and, in order to protect the victims of sin, I have not kept the body informed. For example, I had an urgent call one morning from a young woman in her twenties who was a member of my congregation. On arrival, she told me that her step-father had been on a drunken binge the night before and had attempted to rape her. There is a lot more to this story, but the long and the short of it is that he was the bad apple in the family. I'd already been working with him for a while concerning his drinking. This was the last straw, and I had to take strong action. I immediately placed him under discipline, barred him from attending the church, and helped to get the young woman out of the house.

Of course the expected happened. This man went about trashing my name and trying to recruit to his aid those who would listen to his lies about how harshly and unfeelingly I acted toward him. I was in no real position to defend these accusations because I could not reveal the reasons for the discipline in order to protect the step-daughter. I could only depend on the church to trust me to make the correct call. Fathers cannot explain everything they do. Sons, you must learn to trust your fathers.

Remember, satan is the accuser of the believer. When we let him enter our hearts and bring accusations through us, we're releasing the nature of satan through our lives.

Let's get back to Korah and his followers. Once the rebels were sold on the false identity or impression of Moses and Aaron created by this spirit, the work of fermenting rebellion was easy. The witchcraft spirit had successfully implanted visions of Moses and Aaron as overbearing, self-appointed, and high and mighty in the minds of Korah and his followers.

It is important to recognize that the witchcraft spirit often uses people's words to paint a false impression of your spiritual father.

Don't Give Your Ears

Notice that Korah was a Levite, and leading the rebellion with him were three others, Dathan, Abiram, and On.

Now Korah the son of Izhar, the son of Kohath, the son of Levi, with Dathan and Abiram the sons of Eliab, and On the son of Peleth, sons of Reuben, took men (Numbers 16:1).

The last three mentioned were Reubenites; Dathan, Abiram, and On had no business with the priesthood at all. Yet, they took it upon themselves to challenge Moses and Aaron in matters far removed from their scope of authority. They were involving themselves in things that had no relevance to them. How did this happen? I'll tell you how. Korah, who was a Levitical priest, spoke to them. These three gave their ears and hearts over to Korah as he unloaded all the vomit that was inside of him. That spirit in Korah used him to seduce the other three into following him. You see, these spirits have a committed mandate to involve, by seduction, as many people as possible. This way, when the fall comes, the casualty figures will be high. The spirit of witchcraft can be a devastating force in a church if it remains unchecked.

Once the spirit of Korah had set itself up with an influential leadership to work through, it focused its attention on gaining numbers, also by using seduction.

And they rose up before Moses with some of the children of Israel, two hundred and fifty leaders of the congregation, representatives of the congregation, men of renown (Numbers 16:2).

They communicated and managed to seduce an additional 250 men into following them. By lending their ears and hearts to the four leaders who were now flowing in the evil spirit of Korah, these 250 men became deceived and actually believed, as if it were truth, that they were doing the right thing. They were now hooked by deception, and only complete repentance would be able to set them free.

Sons, it is the aim of those who are flowing in this spirit to seduce and imprison you. Here's a warning. Never assume that you're doing the right thing by the way you feel or by the way things sound. Never interpret Scripture to suit what you're doing, but change what you're doing to come into line with the teachings of Scripture.

I have seen patterns in the modern movies that are on circuit throughout the world. Much of the strategies and character of satan and his kingdom are revealed through these movies. Many movies are made that tell stories of beings that inhabit the human body and soul. These movies typically have a predictable pattern. The being of some sort will incubate in the body of the person that it has captured. It will then use the person as a home to do two things. First, it will live out its evil nature. Second, it will use the host body to procreate and multiply. The end result is the total overwhelming of the planet earth. This is a very simple theme that threads its way through most of these movies. In the end, somehow, the human race overcomes and wipes out the invaders. Yeeehaa!

I've got good news and bad news.

The bad news is that these stories are factual. There really are beings that are living in and manifesting their nature through humans. They are also using their hosts to multiply themselves in others. They are called demons. Even worse news is that, in real life the humans actually have no answer in themselves so they're at the mercy of these invaders.

The good news is that, if these humans would read their Bibles, they'd find out that there is a powerful and decisive solution to the problem. The solution is bigger than the H-bomb in magnitude! His name is Jesus!

Separate Yourself

Sons, listen to me. I know what I'm talking about. Do not keep company with people who are under the influence of this spirit. Before you know it, the spirit of Korah will have his sights on you and will pursue you relentlessly. His aim is to draw you into his rebellion and that, my friends, is spiritual suicide.

> *Then Moses said to Korah, "Hear now, you sons of Levi: Is it a small thing to you that the God of Israel has separated you from the congregation of Israel, to bring you near to Himself, to do the work of the tabernacle of the LORD, and to stand before the congregation to serve them; and that He has brought you near to Himself, you and all your brethren, the sons of Levi, with you? And are you seeking the priesthood also?"* (Numbers 16:8-10)

When this spirit manifests in people's lives, the following common characteristics are evident.

An Unappreciative Spirit

Dissatisfaction and discontentment with what the Lord requires the person to do often manifest as a result of the presence of the spirit of Korah. There is a marked lack of appreciation for God's present blessings. I've said it so many times to my sons, "Appreciate where you are with God. Take your responsibilities seriously. Don't devalue them."

It is a gift to be in a place in which you are in the service of God. The father whom God has given you is a gift. Will you despise the gift of God to you? Aren't we sometimes like the spoiled child who always wants much more and something bigger than he has? This is wrong. When sons allow themselves to be seduced by the spirit of Korah, they become like that. God will never respond positively to this attitude.

Don't be a Consumable

It seems that Korah, as a Levite, was unhappy with his own status and wanted to discredit Aaron (a Levitical priest). Perhaps he even coveted Aaron's position in the priesthood. These other people that were pulled in were only pawns in his scheme. They were just cannon fodder to him—nothing more than consumables to lend weight to Korah's evil desires and plans. The tragedy is that they ultimately paid the same price for the rebellion as Korah did. When sons join their hearts with the spirit of Korah, they also become consumables in satan's service to be used and then spat out when satan is done with them. I trust that, having read this, you'll not be blind enough to get caught by him.

As a servant of Jesus Christ, I am co-heir with Jesus and my inheritance is His kingdom. Those who choose to serve satan are co-heirs with him and will inherit his end, which is destruction.

Resist Covetousness

The desire for the positions and ministries of others is another common attribute of someone who is deceived by the spirit of Korah. This is nothing but a jealous attitude toward the leaders in the body. Don't covet the respect and position that someone else has. The Lord will promote whom He will promote.

I really struggled with this as a young man. I was often perplexed by how some people got where they got. I mean, why them? When I dealt with my heart through repentance and through receiving forgiveness, I never had this attitude again. Even now, I still come across ministries that I feel are not up to standard, but I turn away and keep my heart clean. God places whom He places, and that's that. I have peace with that. In any case, just because another person or ministry may not make the mark in my book, doesn't mean it doesn't make the mark in God's book. Perhaps others look at me and think that I'm not up to standard.

Sons, relax and let God place you where He places you. If you allow yourself to covet position, titles, reputation, status, and the like, you'll be an open target for witchcraft to take hold in your life. Spirits of witchcraft will use these things to trap you.

An Offer

I'll never forget a time when I was flowing in the local church and becoming popular among the congregation as a preacher. My spiritual father trusted me with his pulpit. I was the youngest member of our church who was allowed to preach. However, this opportunity to minister to 2,000 people only occurred every now and then. I used to relish those times and gave it my best shot. It was always my day, my moment.

I was like a revving eight cylinder engine at a red light. One day, a group of people approached me "confidentially." They buttered me up big time. I mean, they sang my praises and told me that I was under-appreciated. They said that I was worthy of more ministry opportunities than I was getting and that I deserved better treatment. They wanted to support me and said that I should start a church of my own in the same city. They told me that I would never get anywhere where I was and that I needed to make a break.

Boy, did they lift my ego on a roller coaster ride! I felt so important, but inside I knew that this was not right. I thank God that He gave me wisdom. I guess it was foundational values of faithfulness that made me say "no way!" I quickly walked away from this seduction.

I had not studied this subject at the time, but I knew something was wrong. I later realized what had actually happened. The spirit of Korah had made a bold move, and those folk and I were all intended victims.

Sons, be wide awake to flattery and seduction.

Gathered Against God

Therefore you and all your company are gathered together against the LORD. And what is Aaron that you complain against him? (Numbers 16:11)

This is what it all comes down to. Moses made it very clear that to murmur and complain against himself and Aaron was to murmur and complain against God himself.

I don't think that the church, by and large, has any concept of how abhorrent it is to God when people rise up against His appointed leadership. When people give themselves over to the spirit of Korah, they're committing spiritual suicide.

Moses said, "*what is Aaron that you complain against him?*"

He was saying, "Aaron doesn't feature here. He's simply following God's instruction. What you're really doing is poking your finger in God's eye!"

And Moses sent to call Dathan and Abiram the sons of Eliab, but they said, "We will not come up! "Is it a small thing that you have brought us up out of a land flowing with milk and honey, to kill us in the wilderness, that you should keep acting like a prince over us? Moreover you have not brought us into a land flowing with milk and honey, nor given us inheritance of fields and vineyards. Will you put out the eyes of these men? We will not come up!" (Numbers 16:12-14)

Accusers

The spirit of Korah will accuse and accuse and accuse. In this portion of scripture, we see how Dathan and Abiram began to blame Moses for an unfulfilled vision. It was up to God to provide the Israelites the land flowing with milk and honey, not Moses.

People caught up in this spirit will begin to go on the offensive. Full of accusations, they will pull every little negative issue they can possibly think of out of the hat and blame leadership for it. They will begin to invent issues with which to accuse. However, God is not 'fooled!

So the LORD spoke to Moses, saying, "Speak to the congregation, saying, 'Get away from the tents of Korah, Dathan, and Abiram.'" Then Moses rose and went to Dathan and Abiram, and the elders of Israel followed him. And he spoke to the congregation, saying, "Depart now from the tents of these wicked men! Touch nothing of theirs, lest you be consumed in all their sins." So they got away from around the tents of Korah, Dathan, and Abiram; and Dathan and Abiram came out and stood at the door of their tents, with their wives, their sons, and their little children (Numbers 16:23-27).

Touch Nothing of Theirs

These ringleaders and the congregation all gathered at the tabernacle. Moses interceded on behalf of the congregation asking God if all should be punished because of Korah's rebellion.

Korah's judgment was inevitable. Believe me, sons, when the spirit of Korah comes at you, he knows all too well that if he can secure your allegiance, judgment is inevitable. God showed mercy only to those who distanced themselves from this man filled with that evil spirit. Those who stood by him suffered the same fate that he did.

Depart now from the tents of these wicked men! Touch nothing of theirs, lest you be consumed in all their sins" (Numbers 16:26).

I cannot overstate this. TOUCH NOTHING OF THEIRS! When you see this spirit manifesting in people's lives, run. I mean, just get out of there. Touch nothing of theirs.

Some people think that because they're friends with the ones who get into this spirit, that they can still remain in fellowship with them but just avoid the issues in conversation. This is impossible. Those people who have submitted to this spirit don't see that they're captive. They become evangelists for the spirit of Korah. They will do their best to convert you and all those around them to follow their evil thinking. They are consumed with bitterness. When you join yourself to another, even socially, what they have in them will be imparted to you. Sons, run a mile away! Stay away from those folk unless they come to repentance. This spirit is like a contagious disease, and you're his target.

*Now I urge you, brethren, note those who cause divisions and offenses, contrary to the doctrine which you learned, and **avoid them**. For those who are such do not serve our Lord Jesus Christ, but their own belly, and by smooth words and flattering speech deceive the hearts of the simple* (Romans 16:17-18). (Emphasis added)

People with the spirit of Korah ultimately cause divisions and offenses, and Paul says to avoid such people. I sometimes wonder what is so difficult to understand about this command from the Spirit of God? The same God who said, "***Thou shall not kill***," said, "***Avoid those who cause divisions and offences***." He also said, "***By smooth words and flattering speech deceive the hearts of the simple***." The word "simple" here does not mean slow or retarded, it means "trusting." You cannot afford to trust the ones who are operating in the spirit of Korah. Know this. They are ambitious for their own goals and driven by the lusts of Korah, and they will quickly turn against you.

Godly Friendships

Any friendships that I have must be submitted to the values of God's kingdom. It is an inherent condition that my friendships fall in line with biblical standards in order for me to continue in them. The moment a friendship violates these principles, it is terminated. I take my eternal destiny seriously and will not tolerate anything that will compromise my inheritance.

The Right Friendships

Let me qualify something here. I'm speaking about the social, Christian friendships in the previous paragraph. I teach my people about friendship evangelism. This means that we, as Christians, befriend unsaved people in order to win them to Jesus. The Bible actually teaches us that Christian friendships can be more dangerous to the believer than friendships with the ungodly.

I wrote to you in my epistle not to keep company with sexually immoral people. Yet I certainly did not mean with the sexually immoral people of this world, or with the covetous, or extortioners, or idolaters, since then you would need to go out of the world. ***But now I have written to you not to keep company with anyone named a brother****, who is sexually immoral, or covetous, or an idolater, or a reviler, or a drunkard, or an extortioner-- not **even to eat with such a person** (1 Corinthians 5:9-11). (Emphasis added)*

Dealing Strongly

Sometimes people in my church think that I take a tough stand. Well, I make no excuses for being tough on the devil! I have a duty to protect my flock. When I see this spirit manifest in people's lives, I don't beat around the bush. I know this spiritual cancer can spread through a Christian community like mad cow disease through a cattle ranch. Many churches have been destroyed by this spirit, and even more individual lives and destinies have been ruined. Sadly, it is often necessary to sacrifice one or two sheep who are in rebellion in order to save the whole flock.

At times it is necessary to deal with a whole group of people who have given themselves over to the spirit of Korah. If you look at things from a leadership perspective, you will find that people who are controlled by similar spirits gravitate toward each other.

For example, if two individuals with a spirit of lust are independently present in a large group, they will find each other. These like-spirits attract each other like magnets. When the spirit of Korah manifests itself in a person, you will usually find the accusations and finger-pointing also coming from those around him. You therefore need to ask yourself this question. *"Who is comfortable around me, and what type of person do I attract?"*

This will give you insight as to whether you're adequately rejecting the spirit of Korah or if you're in danger of being seduced. You may have been seduced already and need to repent before it's too late.

I have no problem with publicly exposing and warning my flock against people who move in the spirit of Korah. I wish that churches and church leaders would take these issues more seriously. If we all obeyed the Scriptures, our job would be straightforward, and the devil would not have access to the local church as easily as he does. It is disconcerting how easily pastors readily accept just about anyone into their flock without ever finding out *why* these people have left their previous church.

Now I urge you, brethren, note those who cause divisions and offenses, contrary to the doctrine which you learned, and avoid them. When people cause divisions and offences, they should be brought to accountability and disciplined. If they show no repentance, they should be avoided (Romans 16:17).

There is a reason for this principle in Scripture. It is there to protect the flock against contamination. Sons in the house, protect your destiny and calling in God by prioritizing your relationships. By this, I mean that you must not put friendships before your calling. Be careful to choose your friends wisely. If a friend turns against your godly values of sonship, I suggest you separate yourself from that friendship.

Lest you be consumed in all their sins (Numbers 16:26b).

Don't think that you can withstand their sin. Their sin will consume you if you insist on being in unity with them. I can't emphasize this enough—stay away!

The righteous should choose his friends carefully, for the way of the wicked leads them astray (Proverbs 12:26).

Be Quick to Repent

Be prepared. Every son in the house will have to face this spirit sometime in his life. When it comes at you, be ready. It will come through people close to you. It may come through people in your church who want to recruit you to join yourself to the spirit of Korah that abides in them. Perhaps you've already fallen prey to the spirit of Korah. It's not too late to repent. Notice that the man called On, who sided with the other leaders of the rebellion initially, seems to have repented.

Now Korah the son of Izhar, the son of Kohath, the son of Levi, with Dathan and Abiram the sons of Eliab, and On the son of Peleth, sons of Reuben, took men (Numbers 16:1).

It seems that On no longer features in the latter stages of this unfolding confrontation between Korah and God. I suggest that he came to his senses and repented before it was too late.

Now it came to pass, as he finished speaking all these words, that the ground split apart under them, and the earth opened its mouth and swallowed them up, with their households and all the men with Korah, with all their goods. So they and all those with them went down alive into the pit; the earth closed over them, and they perished from among the assembly (Numbers 16:31-33).

God's judgment on those who partake in the spirit of Korah is severe. I have seen this happen time and again. It seems that some folk will not hear the Word of the Lord, no matter how plainly it is said. I trust that you will be one of the wise servants of God who rightly discerns the Word and responds accordingly.

Don't let this ugly spirit poison your soul. He is alive and active in the church today. Guard your heart with all your might.

Take this opportunity to examine yourself. Ask these questions, "Have I been giving my ear to this spirit?" "Have I submitted my heart to the spirit of Korah?" "Have I been used by the Korah spirit to bring others to destruction by enticing them into his lies?"

If you have answered 'yes' to any of the above, you need to repent and pray the following prayer.

Father, I come to You in Jesus' Name.
I confess to you that I've given my ear to the spirit of Korah.

I confess that I have partaken in the activities of this evil spirit. I am so sorry for letting you down.

Please forgive me for my involvement with the spirit of Korah. Please forgive me for any harm that I have caused to others and to your kingdom by my sinful actions.

I ask you to heal my heart and repair my relationship with my spiritual father and the rest of the body.

Amen.

Now say out loud:

Spirit of Korah, I address you in the Name of Jesus of Nazareth. I reject you and all of your works. I command you to go from me. I declare victory over you and your influence in my life. I will no longer entertain your voice. From this moment on, I am free of your influence.

If you know that you've delved into this spirit, you must make things right with those whom you've harmed. It is a given that you've brought harm to others if you've given yourself over to the spirit of Korah in any way. If it is possible to re-establish a broken relationship and start afresh, then do so.

PART 3 -THE SPIRIT OF ABSALOM

The operational tactics and methods of witchcraft have now been exposed. These are constant for all the different manifestations of witchcraft. However, the personalities, fruits, and goals of these spirits will differ.

The Absalom spirit is another powerful manifestation of satan. This form of witchcraft endeavors to alienate sons from fathers. This spirit, when successful, is as damaging as the spirit Korah, but he operates far more subtly and deviously. By the time spiritual leadership wakes up to his presence, it's often too late and casualties are inevitable. This spirit usually operates in secret without the leadership being aware of the fermenting danger. Sons are seduced by this spirit and don't even know it is happening.

While there are typically root issues present in people are seduced by the spirit of Korah, even sons with good hearts and sincere attitudes can be easily duped by the spirit of Absalom.

Sheep Must Bleat

It is for this reason that sons must be adequately trained in the operation of this spirit so that they can take appropriate action when confronted by the Absalom spirit. I make it a high priority in ministry to teach my flock how to "bleat."

As a shepherd, I teach my people what the enemy looks like, how he behaves, and even how he smells. It's as though I'm training troops to recognize the enemy. I continually exhort my people to make a loud noise when they see the enemy slinking into the fold. This is called "bleating." The shepherd's eyes and ears can't be everywhere at the same time. So, if the sheep remain silent, they are open to danger. When the sheep see the wolf approaching and make a noise, I come running and boy, is that wolf in trouble!

Now Absalom would rise early and stand beside the way to the gate. So it was, whenever anyone who had a lawsuit came to the king for a decision, that Absalom would call to him and say, "What city are you from?" And he would say, "Your servant is from such and such a tribe of Israel." Then Absalom would say to him, "Look, your case is good and right; but there is no deputy of the king to hear you."

Moreover Absalom would say, "Oh, that I were made judge in the land, and everyone who has any suit or cause would come to me; then I would give him justice." And so it was, whenever anyone came near to bow down to him, that he would put out his hand and take him and kiss him. In this manner Absalom acted toward all Israel who came to the king for judgment. ***So Absalom stole the hearts of the men of Israel*** (2 Samuel 15:2-6). (Emphasis added)

The last ten words of this portion of scripture paint an accurate picture of the goal of Absalom. In the local church today, the Absalom spirit has one goal—to steal the hearts of the sons from the fathers!

Stealing the Sons' Hearts

The Absalom spirit works by using various methods to gain the hearts of the sons. Once the spirit of Absalom has the hearts of the sons, he will know that he also has their allegiance. As this network of allegiance grows, he will become more and more powerful. His ultimate goal is to place himself above the leadership with the new-found allegiance of the sons to back him up. I have noticed a global offensive towards the authority of local church leadership. This offensive comes not only through localized attacks from within the local church, but also from outside the local church on national and international levels. (You may have noticed by now that I am passionate about the local church. I target most of my ministry towards the cementing and ratifying of the local churches' integrity and authority.)

If we examine the foregoing passage of scripture, we will see that Absalom systematically places himself between the people of Israel and the king. When the king's subjects are on their way to see the king about a problem or a need, he intercepts them and offers his help. The same pattern follows in the local church. The Absalom spirit places himself between the sons and the fathers. He acts as if he really cares about the needs of the sons. He acts as if he wants to help the king by taking some of the load off his shoulders. What he really wants, though, is to win the hearts of the sons so that he can gain their allegiance.

The spirit of Absalom will cause the sons to become confused as they are torn between him and their spiritual fathers.

I want to expose some of the activities of the Absalom spirit, who is active and who is, even now, the enemy of the local church.

An Angel of Light

People who move in this spirit are typically people of influence. They are practiced in the art of being "smooth." If it weren't so tragic, it would be funny. These folk speak with the fluency of a well-oiled tongue; they are practiced in the art of a good, spiritual presentation.

I repeat, the devil will never come to you and say, **"Hi, I'm satan and I want to destroy your destiny. I want to attempt to seduce you and draw you onto a road to destruction. I'm here to draw sons in the house unto myself and create my own discipleship base where the sons have more allegiance to me than to their fathers."**

Satan will always attempt to seduce you by painting "himslimyself" as an angel of light. So, anytime a witchcraft spirit manifests, it will always come across heavily disguised as a spiritual entity within a person. The Absalom spirit is particularly difficult to discern because the counterfeit is so close to the real thing that, unless you have your wits about you, you can easily be sucked in.

When people are given over to the spirit of Absalom, they become super- spiritual, always with their heads in the clouds on some heavenly, deep trip that draws in the unsuspecting. They gather a following by expressing this pseudo-spirituality whenever the need arises.

An Absalom Spirit

Let me tell you about my first real confrontation with this spirit. Remember, spirits come in people. People are vehicles through which these spirits operate.

This couple arrived at our church and appeared to be spiritual and confident. I could immediately see that they were influential. They said everything right, made friends quickly, and, before I knew it, were "ministering" to the lives of other people in the church.

I began to feel uncomfortable. Something wasn't right, but I couldn't quite put my finger on it. I noticed that a certain group of people often quoted them, communicating their praises and reporting how "the Lord" was saying this and "the Lord" was saying that. Certain "prophetic" material began to pop up everywhere. When I looked into it I discovered that this couple was drawing people in with stuff that came off of the internet. There was nothing wrong with it. It was biblical and correct, but they were giving my people the idea that this material was somewhat superior to the food that I was feeding the flock. I was beginning to perceive these signals coming from some of my people who were keeping company with them. It's actually difficult to explain. It's as though they were saying that, although we have a good thing going at our church—everyone is growing and blessed, souls are being won, and the vision is great-there's this "thing" that this couple has that would benefit the ministry if we, as pastors, would take some time to listen and receive from them.

This is what I call "crab walk" pressure. Crab walking is when two people are walking together, and one person walks up close and into the other person's space. The second person then gives way to create more space, which will then also be taken up again. This process continues until both people are walking in the wrong direction. The thing about this kind of pressure is that it isn't forceful, abrupt, or violent. You don't actually realize that it's happening until you open your eyes and find yourself having arrived at the wrong place. The Absalom spirit creates this kind of invisible pressure as he draws folk into his confidence, wins their hearts, and deceives them into taking on that spirit's mission and purpose.

I began to feel the pressure from the couple filled with spirit of Absalom. It came through some of my people who were slowly coming under their wing. If you're a pastor, you're probably already identifying with this situation. It is very common in the local church.

Up front they were singing my praises. They came to see me, pledged their support, and said that they wanted to be found as faithful friends. They desired that our relationship become deeper. This, of course, was all part of the lie and was the spirit of Absalom's way of gaining my trust.

I then discovered that, at some point, they had stopped tithing to the church and were giving their tithe to various people in the church on a regular basis. As a result, a number of people became financially dependent on them each month and saw them as godly and wonderful good Samaritans.

As I mentioned before, my wife runs the Soul Care ministry in our church. It is extremely effective and very successful. This couple began to quietly hold meetings to promote an opposing idea to those individuals whom they had gathered under their wing. One of these women confronted my wife with this other program and became quite upset when we informed her that we were already running with our own vision and that we couldn't have two differing approaches in one church. We required her to conform to our vision or find another church that would accept and accommodate her ministry.

The Absalom spirit was becoming bolder as he crept deeper into the hearts of more of my people. I had to start putting out fires. For example, one young teenager, who had been a faithful daughter in her family and had recently come to Jesus, suddenly turned against her parents in abject rebellion. When I looked into the situation I found that she had come under the direct influence of this couple, and her rebellion was a result of their input.

I knew that I had to act and the opportunity came quickly. By this stage I had sought God about what I was up against, and when the Holy Spirit gave me the revelation about the spirit of Absalom, I prayed for wisdom and courage to deal decisively with this spirit in a way that would result in minimal damage.

When I confronted them they became upset and resigned. Of course, the predictable happened. The Absalom spirit attempted to play mind games with me, but I refused to entertain him. I do not negotiate with satan. Next, I received a long letter which I presume detailed all of my perceived failures and their reasons to believe that I am a bad pastor. However, I don't read these letters, and I would advise any pastors that are up against witchcraft never to give any spirits opportunity to speak into their lives. When I get letters like that, I discard them without reading them. I do, however, willingly receive constructive correction and input from those whom I trust.

The Lord instructed me to be bold before the congregation and expose the sin for what it really was. I did this, and only two ladies who were financially dependent on the couple and one other of their "disciples" also resigned with them. The invasion of the spirit of Absalom had been stopped in its tracks, and the victory was decisive. Praise God!

Now that my eyes are open, I am wary of this spirit and able to act quickly before it can get a foothold in the flock. In this case, my biggest mistake was to allow them into the church without getting some history on them from their previous pastor. Things have changed somewhat, and I always investigate the history of people with influence or when I have the slightest check in my heart.

The Absalom Strategy

So, how does this spirit strategize to seduce you into allegiance?

Now Absalom would rise early and stand beside the way to the gate. So it was, whenever anyone who had a lawsuit came to the king for a decision, that Absalom would call to him and say, "What city are you from?" And he would say, "Your servant is from such and such a tribe of Israel" (2 Samuel 15:2).

Be Alert

Absalom purposefully placed himself in position to intercept subjects who were on their way to the king. He knew very well what was going on and what he was up to. He displayed a false show of interest in the people in order to gain their favor.

Sons, you must be cautious when people show a sudden interest in you and your well-being. Always ensure that you remain accountable to your spiritual father. I have raised up and will continue to raise up men and women who will father others in the body. It is a given that I will never be able to personally father every single person who comes into our church. The thing is, those whom I raise up to father others in the house understand that those sons are ultimately my sons. They father those by representing my heart to them. They do not create their own discipleship base within my congregation and become a law unto themselves. When you see this happen, run away from there and "bleat" loudly so that your senior pastor can be brought into the picture.

I, in turn, understand that I am merely a steward of the sheep whom God has placed in my care. I am not an owner but a steward of God's people.

Then Absalom would say to him, "Look, your case is good and right; but there is no deputy of the king to hear you" (2 Samuel 15:3).

The next thing that happened was that Absalom sold the good people the story that he was the only person who was willing and able to help them. In this way, the Absalom spirit will attempt to seduce you into believing that he cares for you and sees your need more than your spiritual father does.

Stay in the Vine

Please note that no one is able to operate outside of the vine. Jesus is the vine. We are the branches. The branches must be vitally connected to the vine. This vine flows in the local church. It flows from Jesus, the head of the church, through his ordained structures to connect to all the body. People may act like they are spiritual, but that does not mean that they're connected to the vine. All fathering and mentoring in the local church must be in the flow of the vine. So, when someone tries to sell the sons the story that they can be a mentor to them, but they're not pointing them to the senior pastor, they're disconnected from the flow of the vine. You can be sure that that person is pursuing their own private agenda. Stay away, no matter how flattered and important they may make you feel.

Undermining Leadership

Moreover Absalom would say, "Oh, that I were made judge in the land, and everyone who has any suit or cause would come to me; then I would give him justice" (2 Samuel 15:4).

Now that the spirit of Absalom has your confidence and you've taken a real liking to him, he will begin to make suggestions of how much better life would be if *he* were in charge! He will carefully communicate all the changes that he would make if he were the one in the leader's position.

This is a good time to refer back to the chapter on the father's nakedness. The Absalom spirit will uncover the father's nakedness before you in order to make himself look better and more spiritual. The young in the Lord are especially easily swayed by this spirit. He openly begins to undermine the leadership and make himself look good. This is when his true colors begin to materialize. Because he has now made deep inroads into capturing the allegiance of the father's sons, he is bolder than before in his seduction of their hearts.

Admiring Absalom

And so it was, whenever anyone came near to bow down to him, that he would put out his hand and take him and kiss him (2 Samuel 15:5).

If you're not careful, you'll begin to experience an admiration in your heart for the knowledge and the superior spirituality being shown by the person given over to the spirit of Absalom. Your respect and admiration will grow for this person, but you're actually being duped. The Absalom spirit will prey on your genuine desire for righteousness and spirituality. This is why he is so difficult to uncover when he operates in a church. The sons are conned into thinking that this person really, really cares for them and has so much wisdom. They believe they're doing the right thing and that their allegiance to the carrier of the Absalom spirit is bringing them closer to God.

By the time the father finds out that the spirit of Absalom has been active in his flock, there are typically a few sons already under the spell of this evil spirit. The father now has a real problem. It is easy enough to get rid of the Absalom spirit, the real fight lies in keeping the hearts of the sons who have been seduced.

Absalom Purposes to Capture Your Heart

*In this manner Absalom acted toward all Israel who came to the king for judgment. **So Absalom stole the hearts of the men of Israel*** (2 Samuel 15:6). (Emphasis added)

Sons, beware of the wiles of satan. He wants to capture your heart by seducing you with a false kind of caring and interest.

In a nutshell, the Absalom spirit seeks to have a greater authority and influence over you than the legitimate, appointed leadership in your life. The moment you feel that someone is busy drawing you to themselves without pointing you to your legitimate authority, distance yourself. It doesn't matter how genuine, right, or spiritually sound they appear. Get away from them.

Spiritual "Shop Stewards"

I have leaders of various stature and placements within our church who serve the vision. They are home group leaders, elders, financial elders, soul care workers and so on. I ask them this question, "What is your prime function as leadership within the local church?" When they are young and immature in leadership values, their reply to this question is almost always similar to "meeting the needs of the people."

However, this is the wrong answer. The mentality that subscribes to the idea that leadership is there to meet the needs of the people creates the thought patterns in leaders and followers alike that spiritual leaders are like glorified shop stewards, who are expected to fight for the rights and needs of the members of the spiritual union called the local church. Appointed leaders in my congregation understand that their prime function is not to represent the congregation to me but to represent me to the congregation. They impart my heart, vision, and spirit to the flock and not the other way around. I, in turn, understand that my mandate is to represent God and His values to the congregation. Why am I saying this now? I'm saying this because I want sons to see that when an Absalom spirit comes along, he will try to buy their hearts by appearing to have great understanding for your needs. He will present himself as your savior and will seem to fight for your cause. This may be flattering and seductive, but ultimately it's wrong. If that person is not building your relationship with your spiritual father and working to join your heart to the heart of your father, then you must draw away. There is a snake in the grass, and you're its victim.

An Outside Attack

I spoke earlier of the Absalom spirit attacking the legitimate authority of the local church in two dimensions, from within and from without. I have already spent some time discussing the operation of the spirit of Absalom from within. I will now show you how he works from outside the local church.

Remember, the goal of the spirit of Absalom is to steal the hearts of the sons. He wants to sway the sons' allegiance so that he may use the sons for himself in an illegitimate way.

Something that has been a real concern to me is the way that the authority and integrity of the local church as an institution have been undermined by outside ministries that consider themselves greater than the local church. They have propagated a culture of absolute disrespect for the local pastor and his relationship with the local church. Many of these ministries have shown a callous disregard for spiritual fathers through the way they've used their influence to manipulate another man's sons. Many sons have been caught up by the guise of "spirituality" and "gifting" of these external ministries and have given to strangers what belongs to their fathers. These ministries aren't even trying to disguise their efforts to hijack the loyalty of another man's sons. It has become an acceptable culture to spend vast amounts of time and money on this practice. These ministries consider people who are part of local churches everywhere as an open market to be exploited.

That thinking and practice is destructive to the body of Christ. It is a manifestation of the Absalom spirit on a global scale, and it is wrong.

Sons, when these ministries hit on you for your resources, they will act like they depend on you. They're trying to make you feel that it is your fault if they have to close shop. No, it is not your responsibility to keep another ministry above water. Let them appeal to their own house to support them, just like your pastor has to look to the generosity of his own spiritual household. It would be pretty chaotic if the pastors in my town had no respect for each other and considered all Christians as fair game to support their ministries.

Skillful marketing techniques are powerful tools in the hands of experienced campaigners. Many honest and trusting Christians are seduced by these ministries.

You may be asking, "Are you saying that I should not support other ministries?" No, I'm not. I'm exposing the operation of the spirit of Absalom. I'm saying that you must discern when you're being manipulated. I want to help you see when you are being coerced into an illegitimate allegiance.

The Absalom spirit will attempt to steal the hearts of faithful sons with the intention of persuading them to deviate from their legitimate responsibilities to their own fathers.

Bless Your House

You need to know that you have been placed with your father in the Lord, and it is your portion to be a blessing in the house where you're called. An external ministry may not even know you exist and may not be in a position to care for you and your well-being. There is one who cares for you and lays his life on the line as your shepherd. He will be there in your time of need. He's the one praying for you in the cold, dark hours of the night. That person is your spiritual father. When he prays for you, he prays for you because he knows you, he loves you, and he lays his life down for you. He will be by your side through thick and thin.

When he sees the lion and wolf come, he will put himself in harm's way to protect you. You may not have noticed, but your spiritual father has taken many hits on your behalf. Don't sell out and give your substance to a stranger who only pretends to care for you.

Of course you're allowed the freedom to choose where you place your support. Christians *should* support other ministries. I'm saying that the sons in a man's house must first remain responsible to their prime relationships in the body of Christ.

The Father Gives His Life

When I was a young son in the house, I was battling in my mind with the whole issue of finance and the local church. I asked, "Where is the storehouse? Where do I bring my offerings? Why must I give here?" I guess these are normal questions for a young man to be asking. Sitting in church, watching my pastor preaching his heart out, I suddenly saw something that settled my heart forever. I saw a man who was laboring with all of his soul. He was pouring his life out on the congregation sitting around me. He was giving his all and was paying a great price to do so. He was feeding Jesus' sheep. I wasn't just seeing the preaching, I was seeing that it cost him his life to do this labor of love for minimal reward.

The Spirit of God spoke clearly to me, "Whenever you withhold your portion from him and give it to another, he has to find it somewhere else. That puts him under pressure, and it ought not to be so. He is your father."

As I sat and watched the man of God, a tear dropped onto my shirt collar. God did something in my heart by helping me to see what I hadn't seen or understood before. I didn't have a problem giving again, and my allegiance to, and financial support of, my spiritual home became unwavering.

You only have one father in the Lord.

For though you might have ten thousand instructors in Christ, yet you do not have many fathers; for in Christ Jesus I have begotten you through the gospel (1 Corinthians 4:15).

A Trojan Horse

The Absalom spirit manifests itself in many other ways as well. Sometimes he comes like a Trojan horse. I remember about ten years ago, when I was a pastor over many home groups in our church, a man came along who was a "prophet." I arranged a cell (home group) meeting in which he could minister. I had contacted his pastor and had received a reasonable report back—there was no outward cause for alarm. He ministered, and it all went well.

He left town, and I did not hear from him again for a while. Then one day, one of my cell leaders invited me to a meeting. I discovered that the meeting had been arranged for the "prophet" who now felt at liberty to bypass me as the area pastor and approach a few cell leaders directly to organize some meetings for him.

The Absalom spirit had now manifested himself cunningly in this man; he completely ignored the senior leadership and set himself up on his own. By this time, he had made friends with a few of my people and had won their hearts over to himself. I often stand amazed at how people seem to lose their sense of ethics and wisdom when it comes to prophecy. So many people will throw caution to the wind. They seem to go fuzzy and weak at the knees at the thought of getting a prophecy. The Absalom spirit knows that and will use it to manipulate the hearts of sons in the house.

The more I investigated the more I discovered how deep this man had already crept into the fold. All this was happening without any leadership being aware of anything untoward at all. Of course, there were offerings being taken, further relationships being developed, and impartation taking place, which was creating a platform for this spirit to operate effectively.

I informed my senior pastor immediately, and we called the man in for a chat. He had a self-righteous attitude when confronted and became aggressive. Be that as it may, my pastor banned him from any further ministry or contact with any of the flock.

I understand that this man still contacts some of the businessmen from the church for private appointments when he's in town. You don't have to be a rocket scientist to figure out why. Carriers of the Absalom spirit will attempt to use gifts to sway the sons. Be careful of the superspiritual approach that will captivate sons if they're not awake to the devil's schemes.

Sidelined by Absalom

One time, a couple I knew became very exclusive and secluded. They picked up an offence against the local church and started holding "spiritual" meetings at their home. I was a young Christian at the time and was easily taken in by all this "anointing" in their meetings. I attended a few times but soon felt really uncomfortable. In my ignorance, I didn't understand, but in my quest for integrity and righteousness, I knew something was out of place. I withdrew but many of my peers were sucked in by their influence. I now know that what I had experienced was a manifestation of Absalom.

At that time, one of my dear friends was the youth pastor at our church, and I was his unofficial understudy. He became influenced by these people and was attending their meetings regularly while he was still the youth leader at our church.

It was noticeable how the youth ministry deteriorated in a short time as this young man submitted himself more and more to the spirit of Absalom. I remember the last time we met together with him as the leader. The ministry had dwindled from a thriving, active, large, youth ministry to a small group of directionless young people. That Friday evening we watched in disbelief as our youth pastor fell apart in front of us. It was clear to all of us that he had lost what he had had. That was the last time we ever met with him. This couple had given him a word about a girl who had also joined their group. They said that God showed them that he and this young woman were meant for each other and were to be married. My senior pastor responded in no uncertain terms. He was vehemently against this idea and fought against it. Rightly so.

Despite my begging and pleading, my friend married the woman, left the church, and landed on the streets, having to depend on others for food and living quarters. He became a charity case, and his marriage fell apart. Today he is semi-restored, but he had paid a high price for entertaining the spirit of Absalom.

Para-church Ministries

Para-church organizations are often guilty of flowing in the Absalom spirit. They depend mostly on the local church for everything they need. You must take into consideration that almost all of the people who attend and financially support para-church ministries are part of a local church somewhere.

A few years ago a national youth ministry started a ministry in the town where I pastor. They sent circulars to all the churches. The first circular asked for finances and premises to start their ministry. Next, they asked for desks, cupboards and finance to install telephones. Another request came for the churches to supply volunteers to man the desks and phones. They also asked for youth ministries of the local churches to send their youth to their Friday night meetings so they would have someone at the meetings. Afterwards, they contacted the churches to release their young people to work for them by running their programs in schools, etc.

Diverting the Resources of Another

Often, the manifesting characteristic of an Absalom spirit is that he has nothing of his own. Because he wants to get something started, he looks to the resources of another. He will interrupt the supply lines feeding another to divert those resources to himself. Those resources are most often the sons themselves.

I remember the time I had a young man come from Bible College to start a youth ministry at our church. When we met the leader of this other ministry, I introduced the young man to him. Two hours later he phoned my youth leader and offered him a job!

We had raised up a group of young men whom we had taught and trained in the music ministry over a few years. Sure enough, this para-church ministry asked these young men, who had formed a youth band, to join with them and play at their ministry.

No Regard for the Fathers

I am not anti-para-church organizations per se, but when they want to achieve their objectives in an underhanded way and, more specifically, by flowing in the spirit of Absalom, they are in error. Para-church ministries flow in Absalom when they have no regard for the fathers in the kingdom. Some para-church ministries think nothing of moving stealthily among the sheep of a pastor's flock on a recruitment drive.

A businessman, who was working for a para-church businessman's ministry, arrived in the area and sent invitations to the businessmen who were attending various churches in town. He wanted to start a ministry to businessmen. He completely ignored and thereby disrespected the pastors of the local churches by approaching their sons directly. His angle was that he had come to meet the needs of the businessmen. Of course, there were offerings taken, address lists set up, and further communication anticipated.

This might sound righteous, but it is wrong and ungodly. The pastors in our town are already meeting the needs of our businessmen, thank you very much! In fact, it's going well.

The correct way to approach this would be to show the pastors the respect they deserve by submitting that ministry to the local church. In fact, this should be the approach of all para-church ministries.

Missionary organizations are also prone to this tactic. They sometimes assume that they have some special call that makes them immune from accountability to the local church. I have heard missionary organizations complain that the local church is disinterested in supporting missionary endeavors. Things would change if pastors could trust these movements to honor the institute called the local church. It is not uncommon for sons to suddenly leave the local church on some missionary ministry, the spiritual father having been totally excluded from the decision-making process and his son's heart stolen from him.

A lot of people make a big mistake by adopting a value system that says that the end justifies the means. This is not true. Having God's kingdom as our goal does not give us a license to ignore godly values in achieving that goal. When we are working for Jesus, we can't use the enemy's values to succeed in our task.

The spirit of Absalom will attack the sons in many ways, but I have outlined some of the characteristics that will help you identify him.

Even so, every good tree bears good fruit, but a bad tree bears bad fruit (Matthew 7:17).

Either make the tree good and its fruit good, or else make the tree bad and its fruit bad; for a tree is known by its fruit (Matthew 12:33).

Sons, you must be very careful and alert. I can relate many tragic stories that I've seen played out before me over the years. Be discerning.

Defeating Witchcraft Corporately

When the spirit Korah attacks the house, I can see him coming and take action. When the spirit of Absalom attacks the house, I am not always aware of it early enough. I must depend on the report of my sons. My sons will see him coming before I do. They are faithful to warn me so that I may act. You must be faithful to warn your father and your brothers in the house. This way, the Absalom spirit can be collectively defeated by the body and the leadership together.

The sons in the house must take it upon themselves to be defenders of the vision of the house. The true son will consider it an honor to be a watchman in the house. When the sons are aware, alert, and bold, witchcraft spirits will find it very difficult to penetrate the local church.

Let me illustrate something else that is important to remember.

Stealing

In this manner Absalom acted toward all Israel who came to the king for judgment. So Absalom stole the hearts of the men of Israel (2 Samuel 15:6). (Emphasis added)

A person cannot steal what is theirs. If it's stealing, someone took something from someone else. The hearts of the men of Israel were stolen by Absalom because the hearts of those men belonged to David. I am not ashamed of the gospel, so I am not ashamed to tell the truth. The truth is, the hearts of my sons belong to me. The hearts of another man's sons belong to that man. If I were to win the heart of another man's son through any means, I would be stealing that son's heart from his father. The Absalom spirit steals hearts that do not belong to him. He goes around the church looking for hearts to steal so that he can use those people and their resources for his own aims.

Repentance

If you have been involved in a relationship with the spirit of Absalom, you must deal decisively with this sin. The way to do it is to repent, cut those ties, and turn away from that relationship.

If you need to do this, pray this prayer with me now.

Father, I come to you in the Name of Jesus.

I repent for submitting myself to the Absalom spirit. Please forgive me and cleanse me from all unrighteousness.

Father, clear my mind of every lie I have believed and set me free from any hold that the spirit of Absalom has had over my thinking.

I further ask you to give me great discernment whenever the Absalom spirit comes my way in the future.

Help me to clearly see his maneuvers, and please give me the grace to withstand his onslaught. I thank you for the victory.

Amen.

Now say out loud:

Absalom spirit, I address you in the name of Jesus Christ. I break every tie that I have made with you. I sever your influence over me and reject your voice. I take back self-control over my mind in the name of Jesus.

Conclusion

In writing this book, I have tried to be as transparent and upright with you as possible. I have opened my heart to give you the truth as frankly as I could. I have shared my own emotions and pain. I have relived some difficult times and some good times so that you could see into a realm that perhaps you've not been aware of until now.

I trust that, with the help and guidance of the Holy Spirit, you will take time to meditate and ponder on these issues. Ask yourself pertinent questions. Be real. Examine your heart, and face the truth of where you're at.

God loves you so much and wants to bless you more than you can possibly desire to be blessed. There is a great future and destiny for your life on the horizon. If you look up with the eye of faith, you'll see the warm, bright sunshine breaking through the clouds in a chorus of joy. Satan wants you to keep looking down at the dust where there is only anger, pain, and negativity. Look up. Let go, and let God have His way in your life. This is often so difficult to do but you can trust God completely, without fear. He will never let go of you, precious one.

If I told you I love you, would you believe me? If I told you I understand your heart because of what you're wrestling with now, would you believe me? You might say, "Jerome, how can you say these things to me? You don't even know me."

Well, I might not know your name or where you are right now, but I know your heart. This is the power of the prophetic. The prophetic brings life. It will flow through a song, a dream, a word, television, or a book. In writing *Where are the Sons in the House?* my heart has overflowed through the book and has found its way into yours. The Spirit of prophecy has flowed from within me to you. That's why you have revelation.

As I write, I sense a powerful anointing coming through these words. I'm sitting at my computer, typing under the anointing of the Holy Spirit, and I know that these words are going to all the earth in due time. This book will eventually land specifically in your hands because God has so chosen.

Is it possible for me to have such a powerful, overwhelming love for sons whom I have never met and, more than likely, will never meet in this lifetime? Yes, it is. I love you for embracing truth. I love you for paying the price. I love you because I see so much of myself in you. I love you because I see the greatness of your heart as you embrace sonship in the house. You have courage. You have integrity, and I admire you. My spirit embraces you.

I love you with the love that God has for you. I feel that love flow through me, as though I were a vessel, and the oil of His love is being poured out through me to your heart.

Prophecy

As I delve into the realm of the spirit, I see the spirit of sonship descend on the body of Christ like a holy mist. I see healing, restoration, and unity come between fathers and sons. I see the joy in God's heart when sons and fathers are reunited. As this happens, it is as if there is an establishing of an impenetrable armor over God's church that the enemy cannot pierce. The oneness of the sons and fathers in the house is like an invisible dome that covers and seals the house, which causes the enemy to become angry and confused. The arrows rain down, but they bounce off and have no effect. The house is now multiplying and growing in strength as the protective shield of sons' hearts, joined with the fathers' hearts, is unbreakable. There is nothing that satan can do to stop the church when she is obedient to ridding herself of spots and wrinkles.

There is a call going out to men and women throughout the earth to enter into this relationship of power.

Neither the fathers alone nor the sons alone can withstand the onslaught of the enemy. But when sons and fathers are in unity, the house will stand, and there will be no evil power that can reach the flock! Hallelujah! Praise to Almighty God forever and ever!

Satan has managed to cause a deep wound in the church as the hearts of the sons have been torn from the fathers. That is going to change.

Jesus is coming for a church without spot or wrinkle.

Amen

Books to help you grow strong in Jesus

IN MY FATHER'S HOUSE

by Amanda Wells

When Paul cried to the Corinthian church "Where are the fathers?" his heart's desire was for the mature men in the Body to rise up and manifest the heart of the heavenly Father. Spirituals fathers are in no way to replace our heavenly Father or the intimate relationship we are to have with Him. Too many men of God today are deceived into a building a pedestal, whereby, they have to keep other men from either dethroning them or climbing on board with them. Let it never become about numbers, who has more, but let this apostolic move be about lives and the shaping of men and women into their God-given call and destinies, who leave an inheritance and legacy for our sons and daughters to walk in.
ISBN: 88-900588-6-2

TRANSFORMATION AND DOMINION

By Lee LaCoss

Jesus says, "...upon this rock, I will build My church..." In this book we discover many ways that Jesus accomplishes this purpose in and through His people. We are confronted with real questions and issues, and are given practical, biblical answers and direction.

The Lord's "new creation humanity" is called to know Him, and to mature by expressing His nature and abilities as true overcomes in this life.
ISBN: 88-900588-7-0

THE DEPTHS OF GOD

By Pat Chen

Pat Chen will take you on a journey—a journey into the world of intimate prayer. Step-by-step you will walk along ancient paths on a journey into the depths of God's holy presence. Along the way you will learn powerful insights for developing greater intimacy and union with your heavenly Father through our precious Lord, Jesus Christ. In holy desperation you will experience renewed spiritual passion. Chen's powerful insights will lead you into realms of God's holy presence satisfying your soul's deepest longings. Hear the sound of the Spirit as he is calling you to enter into The Depths of God.
ISBN: 0768421918

Order Now from Destiny Image Europe
Telephone: +39 085 4716623 - Fax +39 085 4710868
E-mail: ordini@eurodestinyimage.com
Internet: www.eurodestinyimage.com

A PLACE CALLED THERE
Where Contentment and Desire Meet
By Dr. Kingsley Fletcher

Many of us are stuck in spiritual ruts—feeling that the joy and power of our Christianity is just 'not there' any more. Through a study of Paul's teachings to mature believers, Kingsley Fletcher helps us launch out into an exciting new adventure, to the place in Spirit where we experience the powerful, life-renewing depths of God. Fletcher rightly shows that the place God has for you is not easily discovered. The flesh, old experiences, mindsets, and attitudes war against moving in that direction. It is the power of God's grace that empowers us for the journey. Once you arrive your life will never be the same.
ISBN: 0768430186

THE DAY I WAS CRUCIFIED
By Gene Edwards

The most powerful depiction of the death of Christ ever written. See that infamous day not through the eyes, nor the voice of other men, but rather through the eyes and voice of the Lord Jesus Christ himself. He tells you of that day. There has never been a more stunning, more heart-touching piece of Christian literature to be found in the English language as is The Day I Was Crucified. Because it is His account of His own death, you will discover little known aspects of Christ's death. You will meet the embodiment of the law, of sin, and the world system…even the personification of Death as he arrives on the scene to claim his victim. The Day I Was Crucified stands out as literary excellence apart from virtually any books known in the modern era.
ISBN: 0768422248

Order Now from Destiny Image Europe
Telephone: +39 085 4716623 - Fax +39 085 4710868
E-mail: ordini@eurodestinyimage.com

Internet: www.eurodestinyimage.com

Additional copies of this book and other book titles from DESTINY IMAGE EUROPE are available at your local bookstore.

For a complete list of our titles, visit us at

www.eurodestinyimage.com

Send a request for a catalog to:

Via Maiella, 1

66020 S. Giovanni Teatino (Ch) ITALY